An ENTREPRENEUR'S WORDS TO LIVE BY

R. LEE HARRIS

ISBN: 0615573185
ISBN-13: 9780615573182

This book is lovingly dedicated to my parents, John and Jo Harris. They taught me personal responsibility; encouraged me to dream; instilled in me their integrity; pushed me to realize my full potential, and challenged me to persevere. Mom and Dad didn't realize it but they were running an "entrepreneur incubator" when they raised me. I love you both.

TABLE OF CONTENTS

FOREWORD

I think there must be a business book for everyone in America. And there are countless books about entrepreneurship. But this isn't a book about business or entrepreneurship. No, this is a book about life. It's about how to lead a rich, full and happy life as an entrepreneur. After all, isn't that what each of us is striving to achieve?

If you are a Baby Boomer there is still time for you to have success as an entrepreneur and enjoy a long and vibrant life. For those of you members of Generation X or Y who want to become entrepreneurs the world is your oyster. Perhaps what you read between these pages will provide a perspective that helps you reach the goals you have set. Above all I hope that what I share with you may help you become a better, well-rounded human being who will eventually take the time to pass along to others that which you learn over the course of your life.

Entrepreneurs have a complex collection of traits and tendencies. Entrepreneurship is all about harnessing these traits and tendencies into a positive driving energy force. Yet it's even more than that. True entrepreneurship is a state of being. Are you ready to find out more about what makes an entrepreneur tick? Fasten your seatbelts because here we go.

INTRODUCTION

I am not a glass-is-half-empty guy. I'm not a glass-is-half-full guy either. Instead, I'm a glass is overflowing kind of guy. In fact, I'm an "overflow as many glasses as you can find – and do it as fast as you can!" guy. We entrepreneurs tend to be an optimistic lot. At the same time, we are so enamored with what we are doing that we may forget that there are many other facets to life and can become a one-track one-hit wonder. Ultimately, this leads not to success but to suffering. We suffer. And those around us suffer. Especially those we love.

I've been in the business world since 1975 so I've been around awhile and I've learned a few things along the trail . . . and not always the easy way! It seems like ten minutes ago I was graduating from college and looking at the world in awe. Then with a few clicks of the clock I'm seeing the downside of the mountain and wondering how it happened so fast. That doesn't make me unique. In fact, you may be feeling the same way.

My career in the business world actually began while I was in high school. I started a company, Big Timber Industries that cut and delivered firewood back in the early 1970s. This was hot, dirty work that caused black and blue fingernails, several doses of poison ivy and muscle strains beyond one's imagination. I went door-to-door and sold firewood during the summer and then delivered it in the fall. I even bought a business license so that I would be perfectly legal. Wood was stored in several stand-alone garages scattered about my hometown and when it rained I would take pieces of twine and tie the wood into bundles that I sold to a local grocery chain. I kept real books and records, paid my friends that helped me – cash and beer, and wouldn't trade a minute of that experience for anything in the world.

College wasn't real exciting for me. I grew up in a college town and so there really wasn't any novelty to it. I married my high school sweetheart when I was 19 (she was 18) at a time when you had to wait nine months to prove to everyone you really didn't have to get married. We had a nice apartment in the upstairs of an old house and walked to class. She and I both held part time jobs and I also obtained my real estate license and sold some houses for a local real estate firm. Her parents paid for her tuition but beyond that we made our own way and never borrowed any money. In fact we actually were able to save money during our college days though we lived a fairly frugal lifestyle.

I had my heart set on being a real estate developer and I really didn't want to go to college. I was chomping at the bit to get out into the world and make my mark. By taking every class I could take during semester breaks, summer school and quizzing out of various subjects, I was able to graduate in three years. College didn't teach me anything about my chosen profession, but it did teach me how to think. Immediately upon my graduation my wife was accepted to nursing school in a nearby city and we moved there in June, 1975. I saw an advertisement in the newspaper for an apartment complex that was looking for a manager and I applied. I was hired by a young man who had just started his commercial property management company five years earlier and my life in the real estate industry started in earnest.

I had never even lived in an apartment complex before and now I was managing one. It was 234-units and my training consisted of, "here's your desk, here's your phone, lots of luck, and you're on your own!" I hated the first three months of this job. I inherited a staff that included a part-time assistant manager, a part-time maintenance man, a kid who was supposed to take care of the pools and the grounds, a part-time hall cleaner, a part-time apartment cleaner and a part-time painter. I was the only full-time member of the staff. My initiation was truly a trial by fire. Apartment residents were writing angry letters and placing nasty phone calls to my boss at a furious pace. The grass was too long, the swimming pools turned green and I was a wet-behind-the-ears kid who had no clue what he was doing. Unfortunately all of this was true. I pounded the pavement looking for a "real" job, but fortuitously nothing was available. No developers wanted to hire me because I had no experience whatsoever and none of the banks or other financial institutions were hiring at the time. After three months of pure hell I finally made a decision. I was going to figure out how to do this job. And I did.

I guess my pride kicked in and I realized that I was going to learn the commercial real estate business from the bottom up. I read everything I could get my hands on. I traveled to the corporate office for the management company located in a nearby city and pestered my boss for tidbits of information. Within a few more months I had things under control at the apartment complex and got permission to begin looking for new business. With help from my boss I was able to begin signing contracts to manage other apartments in the area and within 18 months I was promoted to a regional property manager's position. We moved to the corporate headquarters city and I began traveling to different properties within that city and others overseeing a number of on-site managers.

Over the years I had a number of other job opportunities that could have been quite lucrative. But I also knew that I eventually wanted to work for myself and the best place to do so was within the company that hired me in the first place. The man who hired me eventually asked me to be his partner and as our company grew I was heavily involved in shaping its growth. In 1987 we entered into a 50-50 merger with another real estate company and became one of the largest commercial real estate organizations in the Midwest. Our company leased, sold and managed office buildings, shopping centers, industrial facilities and apartments across the country. In 1994 I became president of the company and also realized that the commercial real estate business was changing in a variety of ways – many not so good. Profit margins were being compressed and several elements of the industry were becoming commoditized. Rather than fight this trend, we launched a number of new businesses – generally related to the real estate industry – but we were filling niches.

Eventually we sold the commercial leasing, brokerage and property management units and maintained our apartment management enterprise. Today we manage apartments throughout the country and we have business units that acquire market-rate apartments; develop and acquire affordable apartments; invest in various real estate tax credit programs; develop and acquire commercial properties, and serve the real estate needs of banks and other lenders. We also have a construction company and another firm that provides subcontracted services and performs maintenance service work. By my last count I've been involved in over 200 investment partnerships and operating companies. There have been other businesses along the way. Some worked and some didn't. The ones that worked are either still in operation or we sold. The others we shut down or sold. I can tell you that I've never had an emotional attachment to any business but an enormous emotional connection to a number of outstanding people with whom I've had the pleasure to work with. The financial rewards have been a by-product of having a lot of fun and doing things that many considered to be unworkable.

What makes me different is I was able to chase <u>and</u> catch my dreams while maintaining a level of balance in my life. I've been happily married to that same amazing woman that said "I do" in January 1974. We have two wonderful grown daughters and a grandson. With effort and intent I made it to every soccer, volleyball and basketball game in which they participated. I also met every boyfriend (much to their chagrin), and I knew how they were doing in their various classes in school. Yes, I've worked some very long hours, but I've always taken vacations. I've practiced the principles of giving and receiving. And it's absolutely true that the more you give of your time and treasure, the more you receive in return. Life is full of choices and I've made every one of them myself and accepted the consequences of each. I'm a victim of nothing and no one. And I've never believed that anyone ever controlled my destiny but me.

This life of mine is filled with laughter . . . lots and lots of it. I can't imagine how dull things would be without the jokes, the pranks and the good-natured teasing. I've always known that there was a Higher Power in my life. What I have accomplished isn't about me. It's that Higher Power at work through me, so there's no way I'm taking credit.

I am happy. Happy beyond belief.

This book is a stream of consciousness for me. I don't suggest you follow it to a tee. I learned a long time ago not to emulate a person. Instead emulate the positive traits of a person. Live your own life but take the good that others show you and share with you to make your life better. If you are an entrepreneur you know that there are no guarantees about anything. However, I'm prepared to make one iron-clad guarantee that you can take to the bank. Your life can be better. But only if you make it so.

So here's your chance . . .

- R. Lee Harris -

CHAPTER 1

BE ALIVE

Live today like you're going to die tomorrow.

One of my favorite mottos is "live today like you're going to die tomorrow." This sounds like a great concept, doesn't it? Then why is it so hard for us to put it into practice? Adult mayflies live anywhere from 30 minutes to 24 hours with one purpose. To reproduce. They go about their business with reckless abandon without a thought to the brevity of their existence. You, on the other hand, have already lived much longer than a mayfly. The average lifespan in the United States is approximately 30,000 days. That's 720,000 hours. In even more stark terms that's 43,200,000 minutes. We tend to be lulled into complacency when we think about such large numbers. And yet, most of us spend as little time thinking about the brevity of our life as the average mayfly does.

A goldfish will only grow as large as the container in which it lives. Humans are no different. Living today like you're going to die tomorrow is all about capacity. By definition capacity is *the ability to receive or contain*. Most people will tell you to live life to your full capacity – regardless of its size. Truly amazing success comes not when you fulfill your capacity but expand and surpass it. You have to get a bigger fishbowl. But how?

Create a Sense of Urgency

One evening years ago, I took my youngest daughter to a father-daughter dance at her high school. We picked up her best friend and her father and enjoyed a wonderful dinner. Then the dancing started. All of a sudden the father of my daughter's best friend was lying on the dance floor in full cardiac arrest. Thank goodness another father performed CPR and the EMT crew got there quickly. He survived, but talk about a wake-up call!

Think about your own life. We all know someone who had their life cut short through an accident, illness or even through natural causes. How do you know this won't happen to you? None of us are bullet-proof and the quicker we realize it the quicker we can get on with living our lives to the fullest. For me, that evening created a sense of urgency. I cannot imagine taking my last breath with any regrets. Can you?

I want things to happen and happen now. I hate waiting in lines. I have a 15-minute waiting rule for restaurant seating, for an appointment at a doctor's office and even for going to see a movie. If I have to wait I do something productive during my waiting time. I remember once having a lipoma (a fatty tumor) removed from the back of my neck. The surgeon did it on an out-patient basis under a local anesthetic. I lay on my stomach and was able to put my head in a circular headrest with a full view of the floor. For the 45-minutes that he worked on me I reviewed a real estate contract that was laying on the floor (my arms are long enough that I could turn the pages with ease). It took my mind off of the procedure and I was able to leave the office early that afternoon to attend a school function for one of my daughters because I'd already reviewed that contract.

As an entrepreneur I've created a sense of urgency by becoming better organized. I do a pretty good job with time management. And I prioritize. How? I've become a compulsive list maker. I use a software package that allows me to create individual "tasks" (to-do's) for each item I'm working on. I make tasks for telephone calls, for follow-up items and for a variety of projects. I can put "due dates" on my tasks and order them by due date. I then focus on those tasks that need to be accomplished now. I'll drag related e-mails into a task if they relate to that task, and I'll make notes within the task. In so doing, I create a complete record of everything involved with a task. Every evening, I go through my tasks and re-order them as necessary to meet the priorities of the moment. I never go to my office wondering what I'm going to do today. I create the plan the night before.

Some people block out time on their calendar for different functions. I need more flexibility in my day. Intuitively I've learned the right time to make phone calls, return e-mails, work on projects, etc. I generally schedule a meeting over breakfast or lunch. I have to eat any way so I might as well meet with someone. Use whatever style works for you but above all, plan your day. Years ago I was interviewing a potential employee for a position and I asked him how he organized himself. His response was, "Well, when I'm standing in front of the mirror shaving in the morning, I ask myself what I'm going to do today." This was an individual who was inclined to let the river of life sweep him along rather than steering and paddling for himself.

How much planning do you do? Are you one of those people who say that there's no way to plan your day because you get tugged and pulled in all directions and your plans always go awry? If so, you are in a defensive mode from the outset and you are letting others dictate your schedule. You can't create a sense of urgency in your business life if all you do is react. For many years we had a large contingent of sales people in one of our business units. "We can't plan," they would say, "because when a customer calls we're going to drop everything and go deal with that customer." They let the customer control their business life. They were afraid that they'd lose that customer to a competitor unless they responded instantly. This is an example of misplaced urgency. Rather than work with the customer to find a mutually acceptable time to meet, they assumed that they needed to rush off to see the customer even if it meant missing a sales meeting, a training session or some other pre-scheduled function. Interestingly the topnotch sales people did plan their days and stuck as closely to their plan as possible. And these men and women covered a lot more ground than their fearful counterparts.

To live today like you're going to die tomorrow means not wasting one precious second of your life. Have the discipline to plan what you do – in your personal and business lives. Organizing your time and setting your priorities will help you create a sense of urgency <u>and</u> will help you expand your capacity for life and become a world-class entrepreneur.

Live In the Moment

One trait of an entrepreneur is to dream about the future. Dreaming is good. Making your dreams a reality is better. You can't live in the future any more than you can live in the past. You exist in this moment and only in this moment. It is exceedingly difficult for high energy people with a myriad of ideas to exist in the moment. But if we don't, we may never realize the ideas that we generate.

WSC thoughts. "Woulda, Shoulda, Coulda" thoughts are enemies of living in the moment. *"I would have passed on making that investment if I had only known that company was so far in debt. I should have hired Joe Smith instead of John Doe. I could have made more money on that deal if only my wife hadn't limited the amount I could invest."* These are all laments. And what is the root of "lament?" It's "LAME!" In sports we call this "locker kicking." We'd lose the game and come into the locker room and someone invariably would kick a locker. What's the point? Replaying the perceived failure in our heads gets us nothing but a sore toe!

The past is good for two things . . . pleasant memories and learning experiences. It's fine to remember pleasant things that have happened in the past. But dwelling on them can crowd out the current moment. My youngest daughter's wedding was an incredible event – I still love to recall images of walking her down the aisle. My grandson's first birthday party was unbelievable. We put him on the floor of our kitchen, stripped him down to his diaper and shoved a cake under his nose. He proceeded to make an incredible mess. And of course, I still remember with great pride my oldest daughter's graduation from college as she walked across the stage to receive a hard-earned diploma. These pleasant memories give me energy and make me feel good. But I don't spend hours living in the past. What if all I ever talked about when my grandson was around was how wonderful his first birthday was? Or in business what if I constantly told my partners about previous successes and never talked about the here and now?

The other beneficial aspect of the past is the learning experiences. This is a constructive process where you take an event from the past and analyze it to determine what went right and what didn't. Step-by-step you identify what you want to do more of in the future, and how to avoid any previous mistakes.

Entrepreneurs often think so much about their goals that they forget about the present. I call this the GWS syndrome. That's "gonna," "when," and "someday." How about this; *"Someday, when I'm filthy rich, I'm gonna spend more time with my kids."* Can you believe it? I got them all in the same statement. But, what if someday never comes? What if you step off the curb and get run over by a bus?

You might be saying, "Lee, with all of the planning that you do in your life, aren't you living in the future?" That's a fair question. But the answer is a big fat NO. My planning enables me to live in the now. It keeps me from wondering what I've forgotten or what I'm going to do next. It's like a roadmap that helps me get to my destination. And so is planning.

If you really want to live in the moment, do what I do. Don't worry about anything. Think about and find solutions for what you can control and ignore the rest. This takes a lot of practice and discipline. But once perfected, it is a powerful way to live. There is so much that we cannot control. Why undergo the mental anguish of worry when we can't do a single solitary thing to change the situation. For that matter, worry is one of the most unproductive thoughts that can ever enter our minds. A wise friend once said, "Worry is like a rocking chair. It keeps you busy, but it doesn't get you anywhere." If worry creeps into your consciousness become immediately aware of it and then release it. Replace it with a thought about something that you can control.

Never Procrastinate

Most entrepreneurs get in there, get moving and get it done. However, in spite of this inherent sense of urgency, we all have moments of procrastination. Procrastination is the arch enemy of living in the moment. Every enemy needs a strategy to defeat it. Prioritization is the best strategy I've found for beating procrastination.

Establishing priorities requires a totally honest appraisal of each task. How important is the task to the overall goal or objective? Does this mean that there always needs to be a goal or objective? In a word, yes. Without a goal or an objective you don't know where you're going. Sometimes we procrastinate when we aren't clear about the desired end result. So it's easy to understand why we defer tackling some of these tasks.

To establish priorities, set goals and objectives – even for the seemingly inconsequential. The simple diagram in Figure 1 shows how each task is integral toward reaching the overall objective. And by prioritizing we devise a game plan. Ultimately there's no reason to procrastinate. True enough, some of the tasks may be more interesting or fun than others. But they are all necessary to reach the goal line. If you feel yourself slipping into casual procrastination, ask yourself if you have a clear picture of the goal or objective. If you do, summon the willpower and the discipline to push ahead and complete the task.

Figure 1: The Integration of Tasks Toward Achieving a Goal

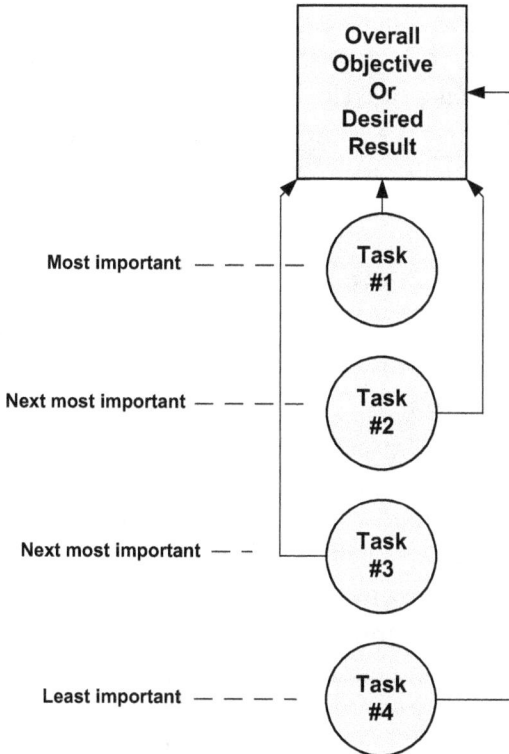

```
                    ┌──────────────┐
                    │   Overall    │◄───────┐
                    │  Objective   │        │
                    │     Or       │        │
                    │   Desired    │        │
                    │   Result     │        │
                    └──────────────┘        │
                      ▲    ▲    ▲            │
                     ╱     │     ╲           │
                    │      │      │          │
Most important ──────   ( Task )             │
                        ( #1   )             │
                                             │
Next most important ────( Task )─────────────┤
                        ( #2   )             │
                                             │
Next most important ──  ( Task )             │
                        ( #3   )             │
                                             │
Least important ────────( Task )─────────────┘
                        ( #4   )
```

Eliminate Wasted Motion

Wasted motion is simply unnecessary actions. You receive an e-mail that you partially read. You close it, vowing to come back and re-read it when you have more time. The next day you open it again and read it in its entirety. But you aren't exactly certain how you want to answer it, so you close it again. You'll "sleep on it." Three days later, the sender of the e-mail calls and wants to know how you plan to handle the issue that he presented. Now you are forced to re-open the e-mail, re-read it again, and finally formulate a solution.

How does eliminating wasted motion help us live today like we're going to die tomorrow? Here's an analogy. We've all seen televised competitions where contestants race through an obstacle course. Almost always, the event is timed and the contestants immediately look for ways to be efficient. Think of the obstacle course as your life. There is no bigger clock ticking than the one that ultimately signals the end of your days on earth. If you could save ten minutes a day for the next 30 years by eliminating unnecessary actions you would effectively add **seventy-six** 24-hour days to your life. You just expanded your capacity for life! What would you do with that kind of extra time? That's a lot of volunteer work bettering the lives of others. That's a lot of quality time spent with family or friends.

When you eliminate wasted motion you have an opportunity to be more productive. Become aware of all the wasted motion and unnecessary actions in your life. This will require some self-observance on your part for a few days. Conduct your own mini-efficiency study and keep a journal of the way you do things throughout each day. Then you'll intuitively see ways to increase your productivity.

I play games with myself to see how few steps I can take to accomplish my various tasks. It's Saturday morning and I have my list of things that I want to complete. I take a pile of papers to the file room in the basement and I know that I need to take along a trash bag for the basement wastebasket. I also remember that there's a sack of kitty litter in the trunk of my wife's car so I snag that too and schlep everything downstairs. Now I'm ready to come back upstairs. My wife needs a suitcase to pack for a trip so I grab that out of the storage room. I need a pair of pliers for a minor repair – so I get them out of the workshop. There, one trip downstairs and one trip back upstairs. Apply the concept throughout the day and look at the result. I want my 76 days or even more! Don't you?

Cherish Downtime

To live a happy and complete life everyone needs downtime. Early in my career I thought I had to pay my dues and put in the long hours to "earn" my way up the corporate ladder. I spent many a Christmas Eve or New Year's Eve at the office putting the finishing touches on a proposal. I felt guilty when I relaxed. When I did take a short vacation I worried about what was happening at the office. I called the office repeatedly throughout the trip and lay awake wondering what was going wrong. As I got a little older I realized that no one in my company was asking me to work this way. No one even suggested it. For whatever reason, I felt like it was the way to get ahead. The turning point was when I began working with some biofeedback exercises that helped eliminate the feeling of anxiety and pressure. Fortunately I soon understood the need for rest and relaxation. Maybe you can relate – most baby boomers probably can. If you're not a boomer and this doesn't sound familiar – GOOD FOR YOU!

I have a lot of energy and drive, not uncommon traits for entrepreneurs. I work hard though as I've grown older I've learned to work smarter rather than harder. And when I play, I may play hard as well. I'm always in motion because I hear the clock ticking and there are so many things I want to accomplish in this lifetime. But with some frequency I hide the clock and just unwind. This relaxation time is one of the things that has kept me from burning out from years of going 90-miles an hour . . . and trying to go 95!

I take several vacations each year. Most of them are working vacations. For us that means that I call the office once a day; occasionally check my e-mail, and participate in important conference calls. I also work for a few hours a day on various projects. It's not all work however. I also read a novel; take a nap; go for a walk in the woods with my sweetheart and perhaps even browse a few art galleries. But for two weeks every year we completely and totally get away. I don't take my laptop or cell phone. I don't take any reports to read; I don't watch any television or even pick up a newspaper. Within minutes after getting on the airplane, I've left it all behind.

I do this because I finally realized I don't want to be a slave to a single dimension of my life. It's not that I've "earned" the time to re-charge my batteries. No, recharging is mandatory so I can perform at high levels. I'll bet you've known someone who worked extremely hard without much else to their life. That person probably rationalized this by saying, "I want to make a lot of money so that I can retire early and really enjoy life." Then when that person died at 35 or 40 you wondered, "What was the point?" I was on the road to being that person before I changed my ways. My children helped bring balance to my life. I couldn't bear the thought of not being around to watch them grow up.

Put Your Affairs in Order

I had a partner who died suddenly in 2002. He was a brilliant man, but he had not planned for his demise. Even though I had urged him to title his assets in revocable trusts he had failed to do so. It took several weeks for his lawyer and family to find the most current version of his will. His estate was an absolute mess and the legal fees climbed into the hundreds of thousands of dollars. It eventually took a full seven years for his estate to be closed by the probate court.

To live today like you're going to die tomorrow means putting all of your personal affairs in order. I can enjoy my life with the full knowledge that I've left no stone unturned where my family is concerned should I "step on a rainbow," as the author and comedian, Kinky Friedman calls it. It's much easier to live your life without a nagging voice (that you try and suppress) reminding you to put your affairs in order. Here's what I've done:

➤ Created revocable trusts for my wife and me in which our various assets are titled. This helps avoid the time and expense of probate.

➤ Created irrevocable life insurance trusts for my wife and me that own our life insurance policies. Upon our deaths the insurance proceeds are distributed according to the instructions contained in the trust documents. There are tax advantages and no one has to worry about where the money goes or who handles it.

➤ Created a family foundation. My wife and I want the bulk of our estate to go to charity and for tax purposes and control elements we set up this not-for-profit entity accordingly.

➤ Updated our wills periodically.

➤ Created living wills and healthcare powers-of-attorney providing instructions in the event of a serious accident or illness.

➤ Purchased a series of term life insurance policies (on a universal life platform). Earlier in my career, I did this to protect my family in case I died and they lost my income. Now with the kids grown and on their own, I keep the policies because they are still relatively cheap and will help our ultimate charitable mission. If I wanted, I could drop one or more of the individual policies (that's why I purchased a series of policies rather than one large one) to save the premium cost. My wife also purchased a significant term life insurance policy a number of years ago. This was done so that if she died, I could afford to hire someone to help me raise the kids. We continue to maintain her policy for charitable reasons now.

➤ Bought long-term disability insurance. Fortunately my company provides disability insurance for our employees, but I also purchased supplemental disability insurance for added protection. Why bother? Most people never need to use disability insurance. But what if you have a stroke, a heart attack or are in a debilitating accident? Social Security disability benefits are not nearly enough to provide even a meager lifestyle for an entrepreneur and his/her family. Also, disability insurance is relatively cheap – especially if purchased early in one's career. By the way, I bought both life insurance and disability insurance when I was in my mid to late twenties.

➤ Created an estate planning handbook, which I update periodically. My wife and daughters know that if I die (or become disabled without mental capacity) the "book" contains instructions for nearly everything from how to access our various investments, life and disability insurance policies, automobile insurance, homeowner's insurance, contacts for various service providers that help us maintain our home, safe deposit box contents, and more. I have the satisfaction of knowing that I am not leaving my family completely in the dark if I were to die tomorrow.

➤ Organized my business documents. I'm involved in multiple companies and partnerships with varying degrees of complexity. I have scanned all of the important documents – operating agreements, partnership agreements, loan documents and anything else that may be needed by my estate attorney as well as the partners I leave behind. The scans are maintained in an electronic archive and copied to CD-ROMs for my estate attorney.

Putting one's affairs in order may seem like a morbid exercise. For me, it's more a part of my personality that desires to organize and plan. I know that my family and my business partners won't miss a beat when I move onto the next dimension.

Action Summary

Adopt the philosophy of "live today like you're going to die tomorrow." To do so, consider the following:

1. Create a sense of urgency in your work life and in your personal life. Become much more adept at planning and time management. In turn you will become more proficient at prioritizing. Remember that you are doing this not just to live to your capacity for life, but to *expand* your capacity for life and then live to it.

2. Learn how to live in the moment. The past is good for pleasant memories and as a learning tool. The future may never come. Tend to your priorities. If attending your son's little league baseball game is a priority, then by all means, be there. If participating in a brainstorm session with your work colleagues is a priority, focus on doing your part in the brainstorm. Don't daydream about playing golf later that day.

3. Don't worry. Think about and find solutions for what you can control and ignore the rest.

4. Eliminate the propensity for procrastination by making certain that you clearly understand your goals and objectives. Then identify and prioritize the tasks that must be completed to achieve your goal. This makes it hard to put off doing what needs to be done.

5. Become aware of unnecessary actions and wasted motion in your life. Then look for ways to replace them with greater productivity which is another way to expand your capacity for life.

6. Understand that quality downtime is critical to being able to live in a healthy and productive manner. You are no good to yourself or the people who depend upon you if you burn out.

7. Make an inventory of what your family and business associates would need in the event that you die. Then, take the steps to put your affairs in order. This will give you the peace of mind to live each moment to the fullest.

Live like you were dying.

~ Tim McGraw

CHAPTER 2

GET SOME ATTITUDE

What you think will become reality.

The average human brain weighs about three pounds. It contains 100 billion neurons that send and receive electrochemical signals at approximately 200 miles per hour. Our brains typically have 50,000 to 55,000 thoughts per day. That's 2,083 to 2,292 thoughts per hour and 35 to 38 thoughts per minute. What amazing statistics these are! Now listen to this. A computer technician, Keeno Gregory, estimates that our brains contain 5 million megabytes of storage space. The processing power of the average brain is about 10 quadrillion instructions per second. The world's fastest computer can process at only a fraction of this speed.

Suffice it to say that the human mind is probably the most sophisticated and powerful machine in the universe. So it stands to reason that we also don't fully understand just how sophisticated and powerful our brains truly are. There's been an ongoing debate as to just what percentage of our brains we actually use. Conventional wisdom pegs it at 10% to 20% - but 10% to 20% of what? In fact, if as Nobel-prize winner Sir John Eccles believed, we have infinite potential in our brains then how do you measure a percentage of infinity? Kind of makes your head want to explode.

The human mind is the key to the way we live our lives. It is the key to how we succeed or fail. I reject the notion that external influences beyond our control have anything to do with the course of our existence. Instead, I fully embrace the belief that our mind is so powerful that we have the ability to plot the direction we take.

Our brains are so incredibly powerful that what we think will become reality. For that reason, we must train ourselves to think thoughts that bring us happiness and satisfaction. This philosophy is called the Law of Attraction. A web site, http://altered-mind.com provides the following insight about the Law of Attraction:

> *"The Law of Attraction attracts to you everything you need, according to the nature of your thoughts. Your environment and financial condition are the perfect reflection of your habitual thinking. Like attracts like defines the Law of Attraction. It is our thoughts plus our feelings that 'attract like unto themselves.' Negative thoughts and feelings remind us that we're about to attract something to ourselves that we don't want. Positive thoughts and feelings are reassurances that we are, in fact, attracting something to ourselves that we <u>do</u> want. You will get what you think about - what you focus on. If you focus your thoughts on what you don't have, you will attract more 'don't-have' situations into your life. If you focus on lack, you will get more lack and not what you want."*

Vision, Mission and Values

In our businesses we create Vision, Mission and Values. Yet many of us fail to do the same thing for our personal lives.

➢ A Vision is what we look like when we "get there."

➢ A Mission is who we are and what we do for whom.

➢ Values are our core principles that we embrace and defend.

Vision

Dr. Linda Phillips-Jones, a licensed psychologist, mentoring consultant, author and researcher writes, the following:

> *Numerous experts on leadership and personal development emphasize how vital it is for you to craft your own personal vision for your life. Warren Bennis, Stephen Covey, Peter Senge, and others point out that a powerful vision can help you succeed far beyond where you'd be without one. That vision can propel you and inspire those around you to reach their own dreams. If you don't identify your vision, others will plan and direct your life for you. I've worked with too many individuals who late in their lives said, "If only. . . ." You don't have to be one of them.*

> *Senge defines vision as what you want to create of yourself and the world around you. What does your vision include? Making a vital change in an area such as health, technology, or the environment? Raising happy, well-adjusted children? Writing a book? Owning your own business? Living on a beach? Being very fit and healthy? Visiting every continent? Helping others with their spiritual development? What are you good at? What do you love to do? What aren't you good at now, but you'd like to be? All of these important questions are part of identifying your personal vision.*

Mission

In his book, *The Seven Habits of Highly Effective People*, Stephen Covey writes:

An empowering Mission Statement:

➢ Represents the deepest and best within you. It comes out of a solid connection with your deep inner life.

➢ Is the fulfillment of your own unique gift. It's the expression of your unique capacity to contribute.

➤ Addresses and integrates the four fundamental human needs and capacities in the physical, social/emotional, mental and spiritual dimensions.

➤ Deals with all the significant roles in your life. It represents a lifetime balance of personal, family, work and community – whatever roles you feel are yours to fill.

➤ Is written to inspire you-not to impress anyone else. It communicates to you and inspires you on the most essential level."

Creating a Personal Mission Statement is one of the most powerful and significant things you can do to take leadership of your life. In it you will identify the most important roles, relationships, and things in your life; who you want to be; what you want to do; to whom and what you want to give your life, the principles you want to anchor your life and the legacy you want to leave. All the goals and decisions you will make in the future will be based upon your mission.

Values

Take a piece of paper and write down the names of ten people you admire most. They can be living, dead or even fictitious. Then, write down three qualities you admire in each of those people. Words you use might include integrity, courageous, optimistic, intelligent, funny, driven, compassionate, creative, and calm, among others. Finally, circle the recurring qualities. What do these words represent? These are the values that you hold for yourself.

Your Vision, Mission and Values are inextricably linked and are essential to the Law of Attraction. They form the nucleus for the good that you want to attract into your life.

Putting the Law of Attraction into Practice

Every other person in North America has written a how-to book about positive attitudes. Obviously there are many approaches. The key is actually finding what works for you. Test-drive an idea until you find something that produces the desired results.

The Law of Attraction is always there. It is a constant. You must decide if and when you want to tap into it. If you can immerse yourself in the Law of Attraction on a continuous basis your life will be richer than you can ever imagine. Thus, this becomes the challenge for most people. How do we stay in the flow and not be drawn away by negative thinking, doubt and defeat?

Which is the more powerful statement?

1. What a great presentation we just made! I want Mr. Big as our new client and am going to do whatever it takes to land him.

2. I see Mr. Big as our new client, thrilled with the outstanding service we are providing.

The first statement exudes enthusiasm but the second statement is actually more powerful from a psychological standpoint. Why? Because we are already visualizing Mr. Big as our new client we can visualize that he is thrilled with our service. In the first statement we're on the outside looking in. In the second statement, we already see ourselves on the inside.

Visualization is a critical tool for realizing the Law of Attraction. To understand how to use visualization effectively we need to understand our three levels of consciousness; the Subconscious, the Conscious and the Super-Conscious. Our Subconscious is an accumulation of our past experiences, a collection point for all that we have learned and observed. Our Conscious mind interprets and filters the barrage of daily data and makes judgments accordingly. The Super-Conscious mind is unlimited and has infinite potential. This mind state is omnipresent. As Chuck Danes, author of numerous personal empowerment/self-development works puts it, "whatever can be conceptualized in mind whether physical or otherwise already exists within the Super-Conscious mind as an already existing fact, and only requires the correct *focus of consciousness to make it a physical reality*." (Italics added for emphasis).

In order to visualize what we wish to become reality we need to access our Super-Conscious. Now, back to the two statements presented earlier. 1) What a great presentation we just made! I want Mr. Big as our new client and am going to do whatever it takes to land him; and 2) I see Mr. Big as our new client, thrilled with the outstanding service we are providing. The second statement, when envisioned in the Super-Conscious mind already represents reality. The process of visualizing reality through the Super-Conscious mind is at the core of the Law of Attraction. Making the second statement as simply a Conscious thought is just another statement. But when we absolutely see things in our mind's eye as already existing in reality, we are tapping into the Law of Attraction and there is no way to stop it from materializing. Why? Because as human beings we are created to receive all good. This is something I truly believe. The only reason we don't always receive our good all of the time is because we make a CONSCIOUS choice not to. So, we have to get our Conscious mind out of the way and use our Super-Conscious mind to stay tapped into the Law of Attraction. Figure 1 depicts the three-states of mind.

Figure 1: The Three States of Mind

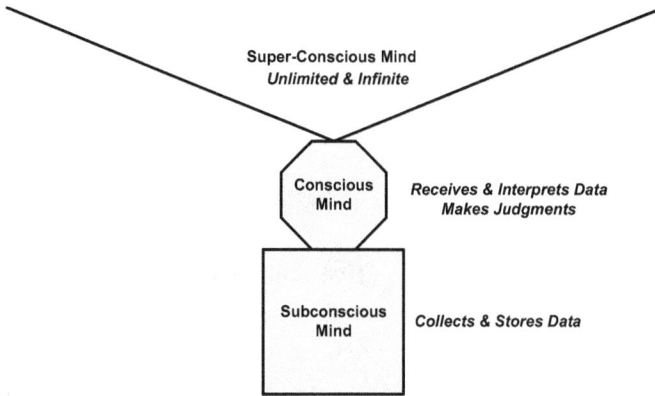

Super-Conscious Mind
Unlimited & Infinite

Conscious Mind — *Receives & Interprets Data Makes Judgments*

Subconscious Mind — *Collects & Stores Data*

Here's the deal. If we grasp the concept of the Law of Attraction and allow our Super-Conscious mind to tap into our limitless potential, we're well on our way to receiving our good every day. So how do I make visualization work for me in my Super-Conscious mind? Here are some steps to consider.

1.   Always, always, always stay positive. Ralph Waldo Emerson once said, *"Your own mind is a sacred enclosure into which nothing harmful can enter except by your permission."* When a negative thought creeps into your Conscious mind, recognize it for what it is, release it and then replace it with a positive thought. For example, suppose you just hung up the phone and learned that one of your customers is unhappy. In the Conscious mind you may think, *"Uh-oh, we're going to lose a customer."* Immediately recognize the negative thought and banish it from your mind. Replace it with the following thought, *"I have a fabulous opportunity to re-connect with this customer and win his business for years to come."* I cannot overemphasize how vital it is not to succumb to negative thoughts. I'm not aware of anything good that ever came out of my negative thoughts. But all kinds of good things have come from my positive stream of consciousness. Practice, practice, practice. You may think this is goofy but it's not. It takes considerable mind-strength to

always, always, always stay positive. Being positive is that key element to tapping into the Law of Attraction.

2.   Affirmations are an excellent way to stay positive. Affirmations are a way of patterning your Conscious mind to focus on the positive. If your Conscious mind only receives positive data, then your Subconscious mind will collect and store only that positive data.

What about all that old negative data that is already stored in your Subconscious? This is where the practice, practice, practice comes into play. Eventually the positive re-patterning of your Subconscious mind will wear away the negative data. If you are 40 years old and have 40 years of negative thoughts stored in your Subconscious, it won't take another 40 years to erase them. But it may take months and even years of practice.

Here are some positive affirmations that I use.

> ➢   I am prosperous and see my life overflowing with abundance.

> ➢   I am the picture of perfect health and wellbeing.

> ➢   My mind is clear and I am receptive to receiving my good.

> ➢   I am confident and centered in daily affairs.

> ➢   I love life and life loves me.

Notice there isn't one single word of negativity in any of these statements. A statement such as, *"I am free from worry and negative thoughts"* isn't a positive affirmation because we are acknowledging worry and negative thoughts. This statement gives power at some level to worry and negativity. Here's another one, *"My business will not fail."* This is full of negativity. Instead try, *"I see my business prospering to infinite levels of possibility."*

3.   Did you know that comedian Jim Carrey wrote a check to himself for $10 million when he was completely broke, and dated it five years into the future? Now he earns more than $20 million per film. Michael Jordan, Jack Nicklaus and Wayne Gretzky all used visualization to enhance their professional careers. Corporate executives with IBM, Autodesk and Yahoo! use visualization tools to make them better leaders. Scott Adams, the creator of the comic strip *Dilbert* wrote down 15 times in a row every day what he wanted. *"Within a few weeks, coincidences started to happen to me,"* wrote Adams. *"Amazing coincidences, strings of them. I won't mention the specific goal I was working on, as it was a private matter, but within a few months the goal was accomplished exactly as I had written it."* We've all heard about visualization but exactly what is it and how does it apply to the Law of Attraction?

4.   Visualizing is an active exercise whereby we see ourselves achieving what we desire. It is actually a first-person mental image that projects us into the end result we are envisioning. We initially focus the Conscious mind to visualize, however the real power comes in moving this visualization to the Super-Conscious mind, for that is where unlimited opportunities await. All aspects of the visualization process are positive. You will only see the good that you desire.

Let's take it step-by-step. First sit comfortably with your feet flat on the floor and your hands in your lap. Close your eyes and take several deep cleansing breaths. Bring a warm image to your Conscious mind. You do this for two reasons. First you want to clear your mind of clutter. And second, you want to create a positive environment in which to visualize. I like to see myself sitting on a cliff on a Caribbean island looking at an amazing sunset over the ocean. Next, see your goal. Perhaps it is a material object – let's say that it's a 57-foot Beneteau Flagship Series sailboat. See the boat with its 76'9" mast towering above the water and the sun glistening off its teak decks. Now, see yourself at the helm, the wind in your hair and the spray gently touching your face. You glide effortlessly along the sea running downwind at 11 knots. An incredible multi-colored spinnaker billows from the.

As you turn slightly you catch a glimpse of your wife. She smiles radiantly and you know that she is eternally happy in this moment with you and the boat.

In your vision, you must put yourself on that boat. It's not someone else. It is you, right there in the **NOW** moment piloting that beautiful sailboat. This isn't a future event that you are seeing. It is happening at this very instant. In visualization, you want to try and engage each of the five senses; touch, smell, taste, sight and sound. Doing so forces you to be there right in the middle of things. When you are finished visualizing, go right to the computer and download all of the information you can find about the Beneteau Flagship Series 57. Print a color photograph of **your** boat, frame it and hang it on the wall in your office. Visualize yourself on that boat every single day. When will you get that boat? I have no idea. I just know that if you believe strongly enough, you will be shown the way financially and otherwise to someday own this boat.

Some might say that visualization is akin to daydreaming. But true visualization is not an idle dream; visualization is a concrete way to create reality. I use visualization constantly in my personal and business lives. Every night before I go to sleep I visualize something that I want to accomplish. That image is especially effective because it becomes imprinted in my Subconscious mind before I drift off.

Visualization is the Law of Attraction at work. Part of the definition of the Law of Attraction is: *Your environment and financial condition are the perfect reflection of your habitual thinking.* Visualizing your good is creating positive energy that begets positive results.

But you can do much more with visualization. Why visualize a Beneteau Flagship Series 57 sailboat? Instead why not visualize a Feadship Royal DeVries 168 foot luxury motor yacht? Read on.

Think Big and Then Think Bigger

I love to think big. And then I move on to thinking even bigger. Pushing the envelope is my thing. Sometimes this gets a bit uncomfortable for the people around me. But they get over it. For me, thinking big is all about moving my visualization into the Super-Conscious mind. You may recall that the Super-Conscious mind is unlimited and infinite in its possibilities. That's where I want to be. Because that is the source of my ideas. Albert Einstein was one of our most notable big-thinkers. As a theoretical physicist this meant that he only had one way to think and that was really big. Anyone who makes a discovery such as the General Theory of Relativity had to be thinking bigger than ever before.

Thinking big and bigger is based on the premise that everything is possible. Only our choices limit us. Do we choose to allow ourselves to be confined by our Conscious mind or do we choose to explore limitless opportunities through our Super-Conscious mind? The world is full of big ideas and big thinkers. How did Bill Gates and Paul Allen develop Microsoft's Windows Operating System without thinking really big? How did Meg Whitman lead eBay from a small auction website with 30 employees into a global powerhouse without thinking big? What about Larry Page and Sergey Brin, the founders of Google? Our history is filled with big thinkers the likes of Henry Ford, Thomas Alva Edison, Wilbur and Orville Wright, Alexander Graham Bell and George Eastman. None of the marvelous inventions that make our life better would have come about if seemingly ordinary people had not dared to think big.

You can learn to think bigger by identifying your goal. It may be helpful to bring others with whom you work into a brainstorm process. Clearly state the goal and then challenge yourself and your colleagues to develop idea that move the goal into a much bigger objective. This becomes a game of "what if." What if we took these additional steps? Would they result in something much grander than initially envisioned? Repeat this process every chance you get and you'll find that you begin to see every goal in terms of how much bigger it can be.

Figure 2 depicts in diagram form how thinking big actually works.

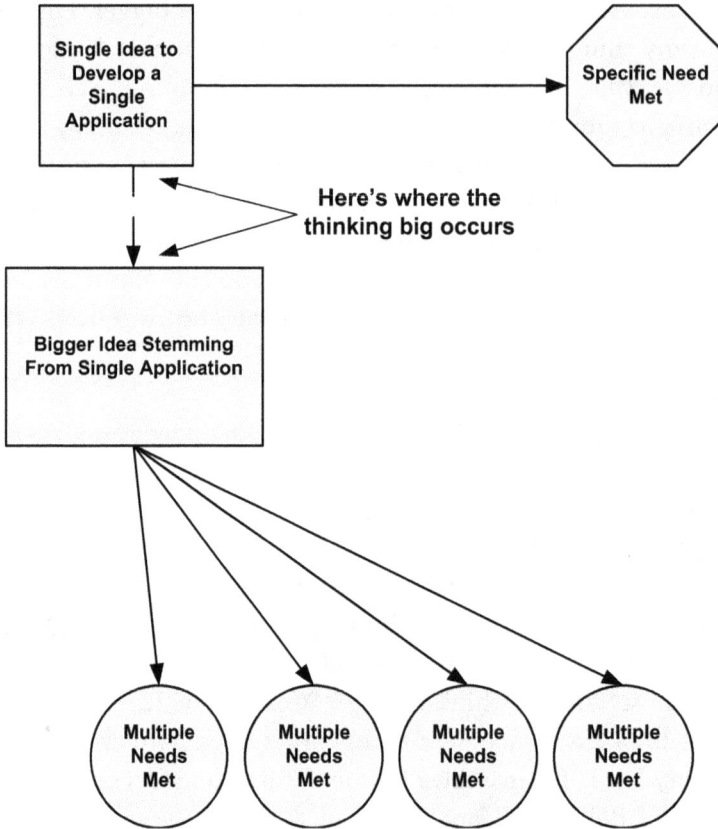

```
┌─────────────────┐                          ╭─────────────╮
│ Single Idea to  │─────────────────────────▶│ Specific Need│
│ Develop a       │                          │     Met     │
│ Single          │                          ╰─────────────╯
│ Application     │
└─────────────────┘
        │      ◀─────  Here's where the
        │              thinking big occurs
        ▼      ◀─────
┌─────────────────────┐
│ Bigger Idea Stemming│
│ From Single         │
│ Application         │
└─────────────────────┘
     │   │   │   │
     ▼   ▼   ▼   ▼
   ◯    ◯    ◯    ◯
Multiple Multiple Multiple Multiple
 Needs   Needs    Needs    Needs
  Met     Met      Met      Met
```

Single Idea to Develop a Single Application

Specific Need Met

Here's where the thinking big occurs

Bigger Idea Stemming From Single Application

Multiple Needs Met **Multiple Needs Met** **Multiple Needs Met** **Multiple Needs Met**

Figure 2
How Thinking
Big Really Works

As you can see, we start with an unmet need. Then we develop an idea into a single application that meets that need. What happens next? We move that idea into the Super-Conscious mind and allow it to explode into an even bigger idea that meets a number of different needs. Here's a simple example of how an idea might morph. Suppose that a certain village is overrun with mice. They are eating electrical wiring, food products, contaminating the water supply and generally causing all sorts of unpleasant consequences. So an enterprising individual sets out to solve the problem and creates a mousetrap. He shows the idea to a group of his friends who are enthusiastic about his invention. But one lady asks, "What will the mousetrap do about squirrels? Squirrels have been getting into the attics and gnawing on support beams." Then another friend asks, "What will the mousetrap will do about porcupines?" Porcupines have been getting too close to pet dogs and cats and the villagers are beside themselves with the veterinary bills that they have been incurring. Eventually our young mousetrap inventor goes back to the drawing board and creates a new kind of live-trap using multiple baits that will capture mice, squirrels AND porcupines. And then instead of selling a few mousetraps he sells many, many more Mourrelcupine traps; makes a fortune and moves to his own private island in the Mediterranean.

As illustrated, an idea is generated by an unmet need. It can then either stop there or blossom into something that meets other needs as well. As the idea becomes bigger it must also be tested from a cost/benefit standpoint. Without this sort of test we'd have some pretty wacky ideas being perpetrated with little or no value. The cost/benefit analysis enables us to take the big idea and determine if the cost to implement it is more or less than the benefit it produces. In the example from the preceding paragraph, if the cost of a mousetrap was $10.00 and the cost of a Mourrelcupine trap was $1,000.00, it is unlikely that the more expensive solution would gain favor in the marketplace. The only buyer would probably be the U.S. Air Force. But even if the cost/benefit analysis may not favor a big idea doesn't mean it should be discarded. Perhaps with a few more tweaks it can be re-designed to significantly reduce the cost.

Challenge yourself to learn how to think bigger than you are used to thinking. Remember that once again the Law of Attraction is at work. First learn to <u>think</u> big and then as you <u>visualize</u> bigger and better outcomes they will become ingrained in your psyche and lead to reality.

The Benefits Are Enormous

"We know that belief can lead to healing or at least improvement in 50 percent to 90 percent of diseases, including asthma, angina pectoris, and skin rashes, many forms of pain, rheumatoid arthritis, congestive heart failure. They're all influenced by belief. We in medicine have made fun of belief by calling it the 'placebo effect,' or insisting that 'It's all in your head.' Yet, belief is one of the most powerful healing tools we have in our therapeutic arsenal," says Herbert Benson, M.D., a cardiologist and associate professor of medicine at Harvard Medical School. Carol Ryff, a psychology professor at the University of Wisconsin-Madison, observed that the paralyzed actor, Christopher Reeve, used a positive mindset to extend his life. Says she, *"There is no doubt in my mind his positive attitude extended his life — probably dramatically. The fact that it didn't allow him to recover function of all limbs is beside the point."* Ryff adds, *"This positive attitude orientation can actually keep life worth living and can possibly extend the period of life you have; it won't make the disease go away."*

The benefits of having a positive attitude are enormous.

1. We enjoy prosperity and abundance.

2. Our personal relationships are richer and more harmonious.

3. We are infinitely happier.

4. We are physically healthier.

5. We don't experience fear and worry.

6. We are more confident and certain.

7. Our purpose in life has extreme clarity.

8. We have more energy.

9. We sleep better at night.

10. We feel more fulfilled about our life overall.

11. Life seems smoother without as many bumps in the road.

12. We enjoy the outcomes we desire more quickly and easily.

Medal of Honor recipient and World War I flying ace Captain Eddie Rickenbacker probably summed it up best when he said, *"Think positively and masterfully, with confidence and faith, and life becomes more secure, more fraught with action, richer in achievement and experience."*

Action Summary

What you think will become reality. To make this so, consider the following:

1. Develop a Vision, Mission and Values for yourself. These will form the nucleus of the good that you want to draw to yourself.

2. Understand the Law of Attraction and how it works. Re-stated here, *"The Law of Attraction attracts to you everything you need, according to the nature of your thoughts. Your environment and financial condition are the perfect reflection of your habitual thinking. Like attracts like defines the Law of Attraction. Our thoughts plus our feelings 'attract like unto themselves.' Negative thoughts and feelings remind us that we're about to attract something to ourselves that we don't want. Positive thoughts and feelings are reassurances that we are, in fact, attracting something to ourselves that we do want. You will get what you think about - what you focus on. If you focus your thoughts on what you don't have, you will attract more 'don't-have' situations into your life. If you focus on lack, you will get more lack and not what you want."*

3. There are three levels of consciousness; the Subconscious, the Conscious and the Super-Conscious. The Subconscious stores your experiences and allows for your Conscious mind to retrieve them and use them in concert with processing real-time "data" in your waking moments. Your Super-Conscious mind is unlimited and infinite.

4. Always, always, always maintain a positive attitude about everything. This takes a great deal of practice and involves releasing negative thoughts and replacing them with positive thoughts. This re-programs your Subconscious mind and to lets your Conscious mind to only store positive energy.

5. Use positive affirmations to develop and maintain a positive attitude and to tap into the Law of Attraction. Make certain that they are really **positive** affirmations without any hint of negativity. Say them over and over to reinforce the patterning process.

6. Jump into the use of visualization with both feet. Identify what you want to achieve and see it in your mind's eye. Incorporate all five of your senses into visualizing yourself already succeeding with your goal or objective. Do this every single day. Do it before you go to sleep at night and when you wake up in the morning. You are putting into practice the Law of Attraction when you visualize the good things that are yours to receive.

7. Think big and then bigger. Move your ideas from your Conscious mind into your Super-Conscious mind and allow them to expand and grow into something much bigger than you originally envisioned. Remember to test your bigger and bigger ideas on a cost/benefit basis before implementing them. If the costs outweigh the benefits, work on the idea until the benefits outweigh the costs or move on to the next idea.

I am an optimist. It does not seem too much use being anything else.
~ **Winston Churchill**

CHAPTER 3

Stick With It

Never, ever, ever, ever, ever, ever, ever give up.

On October 29, 1941, British Prime Minister Winston Churchill visited Harrow School to hear the traditional songs he had sung there as a youth, as well as to speak to the students. When he was invited to give a speech, Churchill stood before the students and said,

"Never, ever, ever, ever, ever, ever, ever, give up. Never give up. Never give up. Never give up."

This is the foundation statement for my belief in persistence and perseverance. An entrepreneur absolutely must have these qualities in order to succeed. Persistence, perseverance and resilience are traits that everyone needs, but an entrepreneur needs them at a much higher level. We entrepreneurs must endure being whacked, kicked, clubbed, slapped, smacked, slugged, clobbered and pounded. If we only "ride the bull" for a full eight seconds we will never be successful entrepreneurs. And, if we get bucked off we have to get back on again and again. Yes, to be an astoundingly successful entrepreneur (and in life in general) we have to be able to "ride the bull" for as long as it takes. Why? Because that's how we get better, stronger and smarter. The experience gained from never quitting gives us a perspective that we can use to succeed in a big way.

How do we develop the armor that is needed to stay the course?

Work Ethic

One of the first steps toward developing persistence and perseverance is to maintain a solid work ethic. While growing up I spent nine years taking piano lessons. I was expected to get myself out of bed and begin practicing each morning from 5:30 to 6:00 AM. Like most kids my age I had my daily chores. Take out and burn the trash daily (yes, everyone burned their trash); clean up the dog poop in the backyard (my parents raised Chihuahuas); mow the yard; pull weeds and shovel the snow. When I was older my parents expected me to hold a summer job. My first job was being a custodian at my church, working for $.667 per hour. I worked on a horse ranch shoveling horse poop out of stalls (somehow I was always on the wrong end of a shovel when it came to animal excrement), building fences, putting up hay and generally getting hot, sweaty and inflicted with poison ivy. I was a Boy Scout and received my Eagle Scout award. I played basketball and participated in track during junior high and high school. My teachers and my parents pushed me constantly to excel in my class work. All of this helped build character and strong work ethic.

My upbringing brought considerable structure and discipline to my life. I learned about responsibility. I learned to try and try again. I learned to always do my best. I learned about following through and finishing what I started. And yes, we had to clean our plates at the end of every meal. My work ethic was shaped by my childhood experiences and upbringing. In many ways I was lucky. I didn't have any choice but to walk the straight and narrow. Others may not have been so fortunate. But all is not hopeless. If you did not have the kind of formative-years training as did I, you may have developed a strong work ethic in other ways. What's important is that you cultivate your work ethic. It will give you the strength and mental fortitude to persist in your quest.

Turn the Tables (Find Opportunity)

When times are especially trying there is one sure way to persevere. Turn the tables. When the general economy is in the tank many worry about what terrible things might happen. They become frozen and inert in terms of making decisions. This is when you can find real opportunities. I personally become totally energized when such conditions exist. When people are fearful and worried they make mistakes. They sell things at fire sale prices. They don't buy things causing the prices of those "things" to drop. This is the time when you use your brain to look for and find opportunities that benefit you. As F. Scott Fitzgerald said, *"the test of a first-rate intelligence is the ability to hold two opposed ideas in the mind at the same time, and still retain the ability to function. One should, for example, be able to see that things are hopeless and yet be determined to make them otherwise."*

Suppose that you are encountering a tough road. Rather than resist or fight it look at your situation. What silver lining can you find? In the process of solving your problem, you can find a way to turn your problem into an enhancement opportunity. Here is an example.

One of my business units is involved in developing affordable housing using a federal tax credit program. Typically the tax credits are sold to a syndicator that packages them with other tax credits and sells them to corporate investors. Until 2007 the largest investors were Fannie Mae and a number of financial institutions such as Bank of America and Citibank.

When the subprime loan debacle unfolded in 2007 and 2008, Fannie and many of the banks no longer had the level of taxable income to justify purchasing the tax credits. As a result, pricing plummeted for tax credits being originated by developers like us. This meant that we had less money to invest in our projects in an environment where construction costs were rapidly increasing. Rather than lament the lower pricing (as did many other developers), we assessed the situation and determined that there was a niche for a small tax credit fund of our own. In effect, we cut out the middleman and found small community and regional banks, area corporations and other investors who couldn't purchase the tax credits before because the "big" investors were swallowing them up. With the big guys out of the market, we found smaller investors with an investment appetite that matched our development production needs. By launching our own tax credit investment fund we generated a small profit and delivered pricing at levels that we needed to complete our projects. Instead of simply solving the problem of lower pricing we significantly enhanced our situation by generating additional profits and cutting out a lot of the bureaucratic steps that came when working with the syndicators.

Get Advice

Rather than try and figure everything out by yourself try to find others who are willing to share their experiences with you. If you fail to ask for help because somehow you believe reaching out diminishes your status, then you are fooling yourself. There are plenty of people who are willing to give advice if only they are asked.

Put yourself in a position to get continuous advice. Find a mentor if you can. If you have your own business, create an advisory board of directors. A mentor/mentee relationship can be extremely rewarding. Many cities have mentor programs in which you can participate. If your community doesn't have such a program then you will need to find a mentor on your own. Start by participating in the local Chamber of Commerce and other business organizations. Get to know the people. When you find a real connection with someone who seems to have broad and considerable experience, ask him or her to be your mentor. This person does not need to be a part of your profession. One of the most important elements of the mentor/mentee relationship is the chemistry. Look for how you and your mentor click. Does he or she listen well? Is there empathy and patience? Do you feel properly challenged? Without chemistry your relationship is doomed to fail. Set ground rules. You will need to make certain commitments to your mentor and vice versa. Decide how often and where you are going to meet. Determine what your meeting agenda will look like. Your mentor should stretch your mind and challenge you to get out of your comfort zone.

One of my mentees told me that she wanted me to "get in her face." She wanted me to call "B.S." when it was warranted. Well believe me, there have been plenty of opportunities to do both and I have. The key was that she gave me permission to do so. I periodically review her financial statements and push her to do a better job of budgeting. We've talked extensively about her hopes and dreams as well as her fears and failures. A strong friendship has developed over the years and we are now celebrating many successes. In fact, the biggest challenge she has faced most recently is how to cope with success. As a mentor I have made an investment in my mentee. It's an investment of time, energy and emotion. I know that my mentee has made a similar investment. Her business and her life are better as a result of our relationship.

I enjoy giving advice and helping my mentees figure things out for themselves. I do it because it feels good and I hope that someday they will do the same for someone else. I don't receive any monetary compensation as a mentor. The whole relationship dynamic changes when a mentor is being paid and I don't think the changes are always positive.

An advisory board is another excellent way to get advice from a group of people who have probably made more mistakes than you have. Keep your group to a manageable size – five to seven people at the most. You'll want to have regular meetings – monthly or quarterly – depending upon the level of activity in your business. Board members should be privy to all of your financial records, your strategic plans, operating issues and everything else relative to your business. While they won't get deeply involved in the day-to-day operations they'll be helpful in keeping you on target and holding you accountable to your plan. Again, chemistry is important because an advisory board will subject you to "tough love" from time to time. True enough, they can't fire you like a real board can, but they can certainly make you squirm if you aren't getting the job done. This is an extremely healthy dynamic and one that you should embrace.

Don't have your mentor serve on your advisory board. Your mentor will work much more closely with you than will your board. Your mentor may become a life coach for you. Your advisory board is all business. They want your business to succeed and by extension you will succeed. I serve on one advisory board where we finally delivered the news to the business owner after a number of years that she should fire herself and hire someone else to run the operational side of the business. Fortunately she had a close associate in the business that was empowered to move into this role. As it turns out, the owner's passion was not in running the business and she felt liberated to pursue those aspects of her business for which she was passionate.

But Don't Listen to Others

OK, so I just told you to seek the advice and counsel of others and now I'm saying not to listen to others. Yes, you want to listen to other peoples' experience and wisdom. But you don't want to hear from the naysayers. You know who I'm talking about – the people who say you can't or you shouldn't. These are the people who want to play the negative energy game and fill your head with doubts.

Undoubtedly they will tell you that you are wasting your time. They may point out that you are taking enormous and unwise risks. Run away from these people as fast as you can.

Be Proud

Pride is that quality that provides the gritty determination to keep on keeping on. From pride comes dedication and a stick-to-it attitude. When our oldest daughter was seven she followed in her father and mother's footsteps and took piano lessons. One Sunday her piano teacher held a recital in her home. All of the students and parents congregated in her living room. The kids trooped in one by one, played their song, took a quick bow and went into to the kitchen to eat cookies. When it was her turn, our daughter sat down at the piano started out fine with her tune but quickly veered off into a ditch. She started over only to have the same thing happen. Finally she threw up her hands and ran out with tears streaming down her face. Naturally our hearts ached for her. At the end of the recital just as the teacher stood up to thank everyone for coming, our daughter marched out with a look of determination on her face. She sat down at the piano and nailed her piece. The applause was loud and my heart was bursting with joy. She wasn't about to give up without playing her song to perfection because she was too proud of her abilities and her hard work to give up.

We need to simply have too much pride in ourselves to ever give up. Pride stimulates us to achieve. When you struggle with a particular circumstance and are wavering on throwing in the towel, just remember how you feel when you become the conquering hero. Focus on all of the times that you persevered and succeeded.

Transform Fear Into Freedom

Staying positive while you tussle with the various challenges you face will give you the strength to carry on. Negative thoughts simply make you to want to quit.

It takes years of practice to get to the point where you have a positive out-look on every situation. But to develop a strong coat of armor-strong resil-ience, you must become optimistic and positive about every aspect of your life. Again, the whole point in never, ever, ever giving up is that eventually we will figure out a way to succeed.

Many years ago I traveled constantly. I spent a lot of time on airplanes every week. I started worrying that my airplane was going to crash and my young children would be without their dad. These thoughts fed on themselves. When I got on a plane my stomach would churn; I broke out in a cold sweat, and I felt like I was either going to faint or have a heart attack. This went on for months. I talked with my minister, my wife and others who encouraged and supported me. And one day I decided that it was time to stop worrying about death and dying. Feeding my fears with negative en-ergy kept them alive. So I turned the tables on my fear. I read books about the physics of flight and the mechanics of aircraft. I got psyched up about getting on an airplane and reveled in the majesty of being 30,000 feet in the air. And then I took the next step. I took flight training, became a pilot and bought my own airplane. I so doing, I turned my fears into freedom.

Avoid Comparisons

Do you ever feel like measuring your success against someone else? Entrepreneurs can be especially susceptible to looking at what their competitors are doing and becoming deflated. How many times have you heard (or said), *"I can't believe that the Super Duper Corporation won that contract! It's not fair. We worked hard for that business and they slipped in at the eleventh hour and walked away with the trophy."* This is usually followed by something like this. *"How are we going to compete when the Super Duper Corporation keeps winning contracts? We must really be doing something terribly wrong."* And finally, *"Our company is really pathetic. We probably couldn't even beat the Super Duper Corporation at Tiddlywinks."* It's easy to see how people eventually just give up.

It is one thing to understand why you weren't selected and a competitor was. If you can truly get to the bottom of the reasoning, then you have a chance to win the next time. But obsessing about the success of your competition is unhealthy. I have always taken the position that there is enough business for everyone. I want to know exactly what my customers want and then I'll focus all of my efforts on meeting their needs. Too many entrepreneurs get caught up in trying to compete rather than serving their customers . . . and all because of an unhealthy fixation on making comparisons. Just remember, if you are trying to keep up with the Joneses, you are probably behind and will stay that way.

Don't Be a Victim

Falling into a victim mentality is fatal when it comes to perseverance and resilience. You are responsible for your own success and your own failure. Playing the victim is a cowardly way to justify quitting. Why? Because you are admitting that someone else controls your destiny. We all have the power of choice. We may not always like our options but we still get to choose. A victim mentality is one of anger, helplessness and hurt. This certainly does not engender the desire to persist.

Here are some examples of what you are likely to hear (or say) when the victim mentality is lurking about.

1. We didn't win the contract because the Super Duper Corporation had a close relationship with the CEO of the client firm.

2. I can't move forward with this project because the city's bureaucracy is too hard to deal with.

3. We would have beaten last quarter's profits if it hadn't been for rising fuel costs.

4. I would have been able to attend my son's school play if it hadn't been for the last minute meeting that I had to attend.

5. I would exercise more but I just don't have the time.

These statements all have a finger pointing somewhere else. And there's another common thread; a clear choice is imbedded in each one of these statements. Let's analyze them further.

1. *We didn't win the contract because the Super Duper Corporation had a close relationship with the CEO of the client firm.* We make a choice relative to how we are going to differentiate ourselves from our competition. In this particular case we didn't **choose** to differentiate ourselves in a way that overcame the close relationship the Super Duper Corporation had with the CEO of the client firm. Had we done so, the outcome might have been favorable to our firm.

2. *I can't move forward with this project because the city's bureaucracy is too hard to deal with.* Of course this is probably true. But that doesn't

mean that the city's bureaucracy is impossible to deal with. Again, we didn't **choose** to do what it took to work through the bureaucratic nonsense. We could have found someone who has maneuvered through the city process before and gotten advice from him or hired him as a consultant. But we didn't do that. We could have developed a comprehensive project plan detailing every conceivable step necessary to get the city's approval, but we didn't. So in the end, we **chose** not to succeed.

3. *We would have beaten last quarter's profits if it hadn't been for rising fuel costs.* This seems like a fairly innocuous statement. In fact, we made a **choice** not to figure out a way to push profits higher in spite of rising fuel costs. Yes there are external factors that influence our businesses – this is a fact of life. But we still have control of the strategies that we can deploy to overcome these external influences.

4. *I would have been able to attend my son's school play if it hadn't been for the last minute meeting that I had to attend.* The honest statement here would have been, "I chose to attend a meeting instead of my son's school play." However most of us believe that attending the play would be the right thing to do and the most important. So we try to absolve our guilt by claiming that the meeting was unavoidable. After all, our families know we must make sacrifices to give them the kind of lifestyle that they enjoy.

5. *I would exercise more but I just don't have the time.* We don't exercise because we don't **choose** to make the time to do so. There is absolutely no other excuse. Whenever you hear someone say that they don't have time to do something it's almost always because they **choose** not to make the time. I would much rather hear someone say, "I don't want to exercise because I'm lazy," or "I don't want to exercise because it's boring," than to use the excuse that they don't have time. At the very least we should be honest about our choices. The best antidote for the victim disease is to always remember that we have the power of choice.

Action Summary

Never, ever, ever, ever, ever, ever, ever give up. To succeed you must persevere. Remember the key steps including:

1.   Examine your work ethic. If it's not where you want it to be, figure out how to improve it. A large part of our work ethic was developed when we were children. Once we're adults, having a strong sense of discipline in our lives will help strengthen our work ethic. Look for new ways to build more discipline into your life.

2.   There is a way to turn every seemingly impossible circumstance into a victory. Challenge yourself to think this way and look for the opportunities rather than defeat.

3.   Embrace the concept of mentoring. Find someone who is willing to help you with your career and your life. If you are running a business create an advisory board of directors. There are many people who are willing to give of their time and energy to help you avoid mistakes and maximize your opportunities. Listen to their advice and implement their ideas.

4.   While listening to advice ignore those who may be jealous or envious. The higher you climb toward your quest, the more people may throw stones at you and try to drag you down. Do not let these people cause you to deviate from your course.

5.   Be too proud to quit. You have likely accomplished a great deal in your life already and thus you have much to be proud of. Use your pride and push to achieve.

6.   To develop a strong coat of armor-strong resilience, become optimistic and positive about every aspect of your life. Work on your positive affirmations. This will help you maintain the energy that you need to succeed.

7. Comparing yourself to others (or comparing your firm to other firms) rarely produces positive results. Instead it may cause you to have second thoughts about your vision and mission. Instead, focus on meeting the needs of your customers. Then you won't have to worry about your competition.

8. Never play the victim. You always have choices. Pointing fingers and claiming that you are a victim is a sure-fire way to becoming a quitter.

Many of life's failures are people who did not realize how close they were to success when they gave up.
~ Thomas Alva Edison

CHAPTER 4

OOPS . . .

Mistakes are simply unfinished experiments in the laboratory of life.

Quitting is failure. Making mistakes is not failure. There are three categories of mistake-making:

➢ Lapse of ethics

➢ Inattention

➢ Lack of information

Mistakes that are the result of ethical lapses and character flaws aren't really mistakes in my book. Allow me to be judgmental for a moment here. If one does something that he or she knows is wrong involving ethics and character then he or she isn't simply making an error. In my book this rises to the level of being a moral crime. We'll talk about this more in a later chapter.

There is no excuse for mistakes stemming from carelessness and inattention. This is where the adage, "if you're going to do something, do it right the first time" is valid. If you make a mistake and you know better, then you need to re-double your efforts to avoid making this kind of mistake again.

As entrepreneurs, mistakes caused by a lack of information are where we want to focus. We're going to assume that we don't intend to make this type of mistake but it happens anyway.

Most of us have been pre-conditioned where mistakes are concerned. In school we learned how to do long division (well, most of us anyway) and the worst thing in the world was to stand at the blackboard and perform in front of the rest of the class. If your answer was correct, you were off the hook. If your answer was wrong, other kids would laugh at you and call you names. As adults these old tapes still play in our heads. We need to re-program our beliefs about making mistakes. This will allow us to have a healthier and more productive view of the mistakes that we inevitably will make.

You Don't Have to Be a Perfectionist

I'll admit it right here. I am a recovering perfectionist. As a high-achiever, it's in my DNA to perform at 110% of expectation. Whose expectation? My own of course. I have always held myself to an extremely high standard. I really don't care what other people think. I have this innate sense of needing to do things perfectly to satisfy moí. I'm the kind of guy who centers the phone on the desk at just the right angle. I don't like to make grammatical or punctuation errors when I send an e-mail from my cell phone. Over time I've discovered something profound. Most of my perfectionism doesn't make one whit of difference to anyone else. I also learned that sometimes it isn't necessary to do things 100% correctly when 85% gets the job done just fine.

Here's why this is important. Making mistakes can be a big downer for perfectionists. In fact, many of us will do our darnedest to avoid making them. In the process we can become tentative, restrained and cautious to ever make any progress.

There is a time and a place for absolute 100% perfection. If you are my heart surgeon you had better be perfect. If you are piloting the airliner I'm flying then you had better be perfect when it comes to takeoffs, landings and not hitting anything in the air. And if as my banker, you're transferring my money, the task needs to be performed perfectly. But when it is appropriate, by allowing ourselves to make non-life threatening types of mistakes without obsessing over them we become open and receptive to actually learning something.

Admitting and Forgiving Mistakes

Making a mistake is one thing. Admitting it is quite another. Some people have as much problem admitting a mistake as perfectionists have in making them. This has a lot to do with false pride or perceiving a mistake as failure. Admitting one's mistakes often earns the respect of others. People generally admire someone who is confident and humble enough to willingly say, "I screwed up."

Admitting mistakes allows us to move into a learning mindset. If we deny that we goofed, how can we possibly figure out what to do differently the next time? To really learn the lessons of a mistake, we must be able to admit the mistake and forgive ourselves as well.

When I was in my late twenties or early thirties my dad gave me some sage advice. He was well aware of my perfectionism. While I readily admitted my mistakes he knew that I beat myself up over them. He said, *"Lee, ask yourself if the mistakes you make will really matter in the big picture. You need to take more of a 'what-the-heck' kind of an attitude."* His counsel was all about forgiveness. It wasn't important that I'd made a mistake. It's how I put that mistake in a perspective so I could build on what I learned from the mistake. If I chastise and tell myself how stupid it was that I erred then I will become mired in that negative message. On the other hand, if I see the mistake as an educational opportunity and then go back to the drawing board for another try, I'll eventually come out ahead.

The Learning Process

"The better a man is, the more mistakes he will make—for the more new things he will try. I would never promote a man into a top-level job who has not made mistakes, and big ones at that. Otherwise, he is sure to be mediocre. Worse still, not having made mistakes he will not have learned how to spot them early and how to correct them." Management guru Peter Drucker from his 1954 landmark book, *The Practice of Management*.

I believe that mistakes are simply unfinished experiments in the laboratory of life. When viewed in this manner we can begin to comprehend the almost-clinical nature of this process. Once we get past the point of not worrying about making mistakes, admitting mistakes and forgiving ourselves for making mistakes, we can work on understanding how to turn the mistake into something positive. For this to be completely effective, we need to create a process for analyzing and capitalizing upon the mistake.

Here's an example. Let's suppose that Joe's in the business of making sausage casings. He decides to purchase a new piece of equipment that should increase his production of casings by 25% per hour. The check he writes for this purchase is a big one and he is confident that the investment is sound. After a month of frustration with the new equipment and numerous breakdowns, Joe's production manager informs him that his business did not experience a 25% increase in production. In fact, the production has actually declined by 2%. Now we don't want Joe to jump into the sausage grinder just yet. He should use the following steps to help him extract the powerful learning process for his mistakes.

> ➤ **Step 1 – <u>Identify</u>** exactly what went wrong. Sometimes there are multiple aspects to a particular mistake. Take inventory and make a list of each such item. In the case of our sausage equipment, several things went wrong.

• The equipment keeps breaking down.

- The production staff was demoralized and questioned why Joe bought this machine in the first place.

- Instead of increasing, production decreased by 2%.

➢ **Step 2 – <u>Analyze</u>** why things went wrong. Make sure that you dig deeply here. There may be much more below the surface than initially meets the eye.

- Operators of the equipment did not have adequate training on how to use it.

- The team did not spend the time or effort re-designing work flow to incorporate the equipment. Instead it was slapped on the line and Joe figured it would work.

- To save money, Joe had the production staff install the equipment. The periodic breakdowns seem to be related to the installation.

- Joe made the decision to purchase without input from the production crew.

- Joe failed to do research and check with other companies that have purchased the equipment to see if they actually realized a significant increase in their production.

- Joe made the decision to purchase under pressure. His new grocery contract committed the company to a much higher level of production. He bought this machine because he thought it could ramp-up production very quickly. He didn't explore other options.

➢ **Step 3 – <u>Determine</u>** how you would do things differently in the future. In this particular case, the root of the whole problem stemmed from the need to increase production to meet the demand created by a new grocery contract.

- We would develop a project plan addressing the need to increase production.

- The project plan would involve assigning different people from different departments to exploring the most bottom-line effective way to meet the needs.

- Assuming that the conclusion was still to purchase the new machine, Joe then would bring in his production team and brainstorm what acquiring this equipment would entail.

- The production staff would help re-design the work flow process to seamlessly incorporate the new equipment.

- We would pay factory representatives to install the equipment.

- We would also pay factory representatives to train our operators and help us through a couple of trial runs.

➤ Step 4 – **Leverage** the mistake for a positive outcome. Fix the mistake if possible and try to turn the experience into a big win.

- Joe should call the production team together and admit that a mistake was made in purchasing the equipment without their input. Joe will gain respect for making this admission.

- He should ask the production team to help brainstorm ways to make this piece of equipment work. You may be amazed at how creative people are when thrown this sort of a challenge.

- Your production team is re-energized by being asked to solve a problem and then being empowered to do so. From what was going to be a resounding disaster emerges a closer-knit group of employees with an even greater respect for the business owner.

Encouraging Mistakes

A number of forward-thinking business people deploy an interesting strategy that that actually encourages mistakes. Paul Lemberg, a highly regarded business coach recommends using a process called rapid prototyping. He says, *"This technical-sounding phrase simply means doing things quickly, making mistakes and swiftly fixing them. Get something up and running - anything that resembles your desired solution. Then fix what isn't working. And fix, and fix, and fix. This may be the best way to do product development in Internet Time, also known as creative trial and error."*

An organization that encourages mistakes creates a vibrant culture. Employees know they are free to experiment without ridicule or recrimination for the mistakes they make. This kind of culture can inspire extremely high levels of innovation. To make this work effectively the organization must establish specific experimentation parameters. They can also create a process so the mistakes that result from such experiments are documented and carefully analyzed to determine how they can use the lessons learned to reach the firm's ultimate objective. I've even heard of entrepreneurs who will offer rewards for the biggest mistake or the largest number of mistakes – again all within pre-determined guidelines. The goal is making mistakes that build toward a successful conclusion relative to a product or a service.

If you want to adopt a mistake-embracing philosophy, I recommend that you study a concept call Fail Forward Fast (FFF). According to Rod Moore of Life Design Systems, Fail Forward Fast is a mindset that says that the more I am prepared to risk temporary failure through having a go, the faster I am likely to arrive at a point of success. This is because each failed attempt is a learning experience that allows me to adjust my approach, take new action and experience new outcomes. For years, world-renowned leadership expert, Tom Peters has championed FFF. He quotes Phil Daniels, a Sydney, Australia executive as saying, *"Reward excellent failures. Punish mediocre successes."* And Peters also proclaims, *"You only find oil if you drill wells."* Clearly the belief is that failure and mistakes can be stepping stones to success.

"To survive, organizations need to experiment constantly with new ideas and not get stuck doing the same old routine," says Fiona Lee, a University of Michigan psychology and business professor who is an expert on organizational behavior. *"We've been looking at why some people experiment and others don't. We find that when managers send mixed messages, people get scared and actually stop trying out new ideas."* According to Ms. Lee, people who fear their mistakes, errors and failures will be held against them lack "psychological safety" and become fearful of taking risks or experimenting. Rewarding employees who repeatedly try new things and fail, actually leads to more innovation and bigger long-term successes. Individuals who constantly improvise, tinker and experiment can to adapt quickly in fast-paced industries where new ideas and inventions are constantly in demand. But the encouragement to experiment must be consistent throughout the corporate culture.

According to Lee's research, supportive coaching can encourage risk-taking while close and constant evaluation designed to expose failures actually inhibits creativity, making people reluctant to experiment or take risks. This is true even when top management explicitly encouraged people to experiment.

Lee studied a major hospital system as it implemented new technology. Even though the management encouraged experimentation the systems penalized failures. These mixed signals made people more rigid, more risk-averse and less likely to try out new ideas. Lee describes a similar pattern at Bank of America. In 2000, they established 24 branches that were designed to experiment with new product and service ideas. However, management did not adjust reward systems and people were penalized for failures. As a result, most employees were reluctant to experiment. Telling people to experiment but monitoring and punishing their mistakes when they do so lowers psychological safety and increases fear, creating discouraging conditions, she says.

Great Mistake-Makers

Great discoveries and innovations would never have occurred without goofs, blunders and mistakes galore. Here are some examples.

➢ A scientist for the 3M Corporation attempted to develop a very strong adhesive. The result was a very weak adhesive. From this mistake evolved the ubiquitous Post-it Note®.

➢ Thomas Edison tried thousands of different ways capture light before he finally invented the light bulb.

➢ Coca-Cola and chocolate chip cookies were purportedly all the results of mistakes.

➢ The invention of Teflon was the result of a mistake.

➢ Silly Putty was invented by a scientist who was trying to make synthetic rubber.

➢ The microwave oven came about when a magnetron melted a candy bar in a Raytheon engineer's pocket.

My Humdinger Hall-of-Fame-Size Screw-Ups

I've learned so much from my own mistakes. Here are a couple of my biggest screw-ups.

1. **Facilities Management Venture** – I wanted to venture into managing corporate facilities. I learned of a fledgling firm that was already in the facilities management business and approached them about a partnership. The discussions led to the formation of a jointly-owned company. They moved into extra space we had in our offices and we were off and running. The individual who was in charge of this operation was an eternal optimist (just like me) and had terrific ideas and boundless energy. She gave me reports of new business – both opportunities and actual contracts. But what I didn't know was that we were adding overhead like crazy. One day walked into this business and saw hordes of people. "Who are all these people?"

I asked my new partner. "With all this new business, we needed more employees," she said.

Ultimately the income statement told the real story. We were paying a lot of people and the revenues didn't support the expense. Eventually we shut down the business unit and my partner paid back the excess monies that we had unknowingly invested.

I learned a number of valuable lessons:

➢ Pay much closer attention to the revenue/overhead relationship.

➢ Set the ground rules for a partnership.

➢ Spend more time in the beginning interviewing a partner and verifying his or her track record.

Since this experience I've remembered these lessons in the process of forming other ventures and have not made the same mistakes twice.

2. **Interest Rate Hedge** – Probably the most expensive blunder involved two real estate developments. We built identical 97-unit apartment communities in separate cities during a time when interest rates were relatively volatile. Our construction loans had floating rates of interest. The lender wanted us to hedge the rates in case we could not lock-in a fixed-rate permanent loan at the rate at which we had underwritten the deals. A banker explained how this process worked. We would sell Treasury futures and if interest rates rose, we would make money on the transaction. The profit, in theory, would offset the higher interest rate on the permanent financing. Conversely, if interest rates dropped, we would have a loss on our hedge transaction, but we were assured that we could to obtain a much lower interest rate on our permanent loan. Again in theory, any loss would be offset by our being able to borrow more money on the permanent loan.

You can imagine what happened. Interest rates dropped which caused a loss in our Treasury futures hedge. Rates kept dropping resulting in even bigger losses. Meanwhile when the time came to close the permanent loans, we learned that the hedge was not perfect. Yes, the interest rate on the permanent loan had correspondingly dropped. However we were not able to borrow more money. When we finally wound up our hedge position, we had lost between $400,000 and $500,000.

The moral of the story is that highly complex situations require several pairs of eyes. I should have had a number of other experts look at it. My partners weren't any more capable of evaluating the downside risk than I was.

Action Summary

Mistakes are simply unfinished experiments.

1. We all have "old tapes" that say mistakes are bad and that we can't afford to make them. These tapes must be re-recorded with a different message.

2. The new message should state that perfectionism is rarely productive except where lives are at stake. Most of the time, when it comes to your day-to-day performance the 80/20 rule works just fine – that is, 80% perfect and 20% not.

3. Admitting mistakes allows us to move into a learning mindset. But to really learn the lessons of a mistake we must not only be able to admit the mistake but forgive ourselves as well. This will help us maintain a positive, healthy attitude about our mistakes.

4. Once we get past the point of not worrying about making mistakes, admitting mistakes and forgiving ourselves for making mistakes,

we can really get into the meat of the matter. We must be able to understand how to turn the mistake into something positive. For this to be completely effective we need to create a process for analyzing and capitalizing upon the mistake.

5.   The process for learning from our mistakes includes identifying exactly what went wrong; analyzing why things went wrong; determining how we would do things differently in the future, and looking for ways to leverage the mistake for a positive outcome.

6.   Adopt a Fail Forward Fast (FFF) mentality. This encourages mistakes to be made within pre-determined guidelines in order to promote innovation. Create a culture in your organization where mistakes are actually rewarded if they help move you toward your end objectives.

7.   Remember that the mother of all invention were mistakes and failures. Without them we would still be living in caves and being eaten by a wide range of horrible animals.

Mistakes are part of the dues one pays for a full life.
~ Sophia Loren

CHAPTER 5

CREATIVITY

Creativity is a way to express your passion.
And, passion allows you to see in color.

My entrepreneurial engine gets revved up into overdrive at the mention of creativity. This is where the Super-Conscious Mind comes into play. A lot of entrepreneurs share the same excitement about creativity. After all, it's at the core of what we do – generating ideas galore, creating things, turning dreams into reality. Some people claim to have no creativity but I don't believe it for one second. Some of us may be able to access ideas and dreams more easily, but creativity is imbedded in each and every one of us.

Being creative is such a positive process, with no room for negative energy. The stream of ideas that flows from my brain has increased exponentially through the years. The more creative the flow, the greater the chance for success. Nurturing a creative mindset in an ever-increasing number of people can solve a multitude of problems, introduce countless new products and services, and generally stand conventional wisdom on its ear. After all, there's nothing traditional or conventional about creativity!

Stimulating Creativity

I'm constantly trying to stimulate creativity in myself and others. Be interested in all that is going on in the world. I read novels, biographies, history, non-fiction, humor and other books. I read at least 100 books each year. I read magazines and newspapers on current events, politics, sports, business, travel, religion, wine, cigars, interior design – you name it, I read it. And then there's the Internet. When I was a young boy we had a set of World Book encyclopedias. I loved to sit down with a volume on a rainy Saturday and just read through page after page. Each year we received a supplement and I eagerly awaited the day it arrived. Today, I can go on-line and access a thousand times more information than was ever available in the old World Book.

Why is reading everything so important for stimulating creativity? Because it makes us think about so many different things. It forces us out of a one-dimensional perspective and pushes us to explore a wide range of issues, concepts and ideas. We store what we read is stored in the subconscious portion of our brain to be called forth in the future.

Invite Day Dream Time

I use long driving trips to stimulate creativity. Long trips are a great opportunity for me to daydream and solve problems or assemble random thoughts into an idea on which I can act. Turn off the radio and let the thoughts float. Be prepared to record any ideas that appeal to you. Don't judge them. If an idea or thought persists, record it. Other people like long walks or repetitive physical exercise such as swimming.

Some people use crossword puzzles, word searches, the physical process of putting together a puzzle, completing a crossword puzzle or other puzzle-related activities to stimulate creativity. There's something about solving problems and the order that is created in the mind to unlock a vast array of ideas. Obviously puzzles represent a method of solving problems.

Here are things you might consider to boost your creativity.

1. Every day read voraciously including books, magazines and newspapers.

2. Meditate daily. Find a quiet place where you can sit in silence and focus your mind into a state of nothingness. Then allow the thoughts and ideas gently flow. Spend ten or 15 minutes with this exercise.

3. Experience the arts. Attend a concert, listen to music, walk through an art gallery or museum, read poetry or watch a play. Even if you don't have an artistic flair, experiencing the arts will help align your creativity within your Super Conscious Mind.

4. Surf the Internet. Use the Internet in a positive way to stimulate your brain. Research historical events, look-up words that you've heard in an on-line dictionary, explore far-off lands or learn how to create a gourmet meal.

5. Get out of your comfort zone. Challenge yourself to do something different. We all get into a routine. Take a different route home from work; eat at a new restaurant; sit in a different pew in church or take a vacation to a new location. You can amp this up by joining a new organization where you meet new people; find a new hobby, or conquer a phobia.

6. Exercise your body. Our brains need oxygen. Physical activity helps bring oxygen through your lungs and into your bloodstream. Your brain will function at greater capacity with more oxygen.

7. Debate. Find people with different points of view with whom you can debate an issue. It's important that your debate partners understand that this is a friendly activity and they should enjoy it as much as you do. Pick a subject where you may disagree whether it's politics, religion, culture or ethics.

8. Brainstorm regularly. Gather colleagues at work or your friends and family to brainstorm with you about a particular subject. Participants in a brainstorming session stimulate each other and you'll find the process exhilarating.

Brainstorming

Brainstorming and creativity go hand-in-hand. Before any brainstorming exercise spend some time relaxing. Clear your mind of clutter and negativity. A positive mindset is helps to set the right tone for the rest of your brainstorm team. Find a place to brainstorm where everyone can be comfortable and won't be interrupted. I always like to conduct brainstorm sessions away from the office. This sends the message to everyone involved that what we are doing is important enough that we are going to focus solely on the creative function and not allow anything to distract us. Invite five to 12 people from a wide range of disciplines to participate, ensuring a variety of perspectives.

The next step is to set the grounds rules for brainstorming.

> ➢ All cell phones should be shut off.

> ➢ Any and every idea is welcome – nothing is too off-the-wall for this process.

> ➢ A scribe will record all ideas.

> ➢ Only one person should speak at a time.

> ➢ No one's idea will be ridiculed or criticized.

> ➢ Repeating ideas is fine.

> ➢ Piggybacking on others' ideas is great.

> ➤ The brainstorm session should last one to two hours.

> ➤ A biological break will be permitted at the half-way mark but no one should be permitted to check e-mail or return phone calls. This breaks the focus of the brainstorm.

Begin by discussing the subject you're brainstorming. Outline any criteria or important parameters to understanding the issue at hand. Use a white board or flip chart for stating the subject and recording ideas. As the brainstorm progresses make certain that ideas come from everyone. With a small enough group, it is hard for even the quietest person to sit by without participating. Stay focused. As the facilitator you don't want to stray too far from the subject. You don't want to squelch the flow of ideas and you do want to stay on point to the greatest extent possible. Keep the discussion moving and don't get stuck for too long on one subject. Again, you don't want to interrupt the creative flow but you do have a mission to accomplish. Encourage the group to work on each other's ideas. Everyone doesn't necessarily have to have an original idea – there is nothing wrong with brainstorming further on the idea of one of the participants. Have fun. Invite laughter and a positive feeling throughout the brainstorm process.

Before the brainstorming session ends, group the ideas into categories. Leaving the ideas alone for a few days allows some gestation time. Schedule a second meeting to review the ideas and determine which to incorporate and how to move forward. Eventually you'll assign the ideas to different team members for further development.

Recently a woman asked me to help her come up with some ideas for her business. Her core business was fundamentally solid but needed to be contemporized. After understanding more about what she does I offered to facilitate a group brainstorm session. A few weeks later she assembled 12 people including members of her advisory board, a couple of clients (that took some guts!) and other business people. I set the grounds rules and kicked off the discussion with some ideas of my own. We were off and running. The brainstorm session was like riding a bucking bronco in the middle of a tornado. Ideas flew and the participation was excellent. I was amazed at how forthcoming one of her clients was. We filled a dozen flip chart pages in two hours and the business owner was ecstatic with the results.

But here's the real secret. I benefited from this brainstorm session as much as the business owner. Why? Because the process of understanding someone else's business and developing helpful ideas was phenomenally stimulating for me. I felt a real adrenaline rush and then euphoria. It's as close to a pure creative stream of consciousness as I can get. I came away from the brainstorm session with a thousand new ideas for my own businesses.

Channeling Creativity

Once you've completed the creative thinking and brainstorming, it's time to channel the creative ideas into something productive. How do we channel creativity into something productive? Teresa Amabile runs the Entrepreneurial Management Unit at Harvard Business School and for the past 30 years she's conducted research on creativity and innovation. According to an interview in *Fast Company* Magazine, Bill Breen interviewed her in the December 2004 issue where she discussed an extensive study on creativity and shared some interesting conclusions:

> ➢ "Of course, people need to feel that they're being compensated fairly. But our research shows that people put far more value on a work environment where creativity is supported, valued, and recognized. People want the opportunity to deeply engage in their work and make real progress."

> ➢ "People were the least creative when they were fighting the clock. Time pressure stifles creativity because people can't deeply engage with the problem. Creativity requires an incubation period; people need time to soak in a problem and let the ideas bubble up."

> ➤ "Creativity is positively associated with joy and love and negatively associated with anger, fear, and anxiety."

> ➤ "Creativity takes a hit when people in a work group compete instead of collaborate. The most creative teams are those that have the confidence to share and debate ideas."

Obviously we need to create the right environment to nurture creativity and celebrate its importance. And then the key is to move creativity into action. It's time to put the painting on the canvas so to speak.

To move to action, the creative exercise needs what I call a "**linear translation.**" which brings the left-brain into play. This is where we take our random and intuitive thoughts and bring them into a logical, sequential and rational mode. One of the best ways to accomplish this is through a Project Plan. The Project Plan takes each idea from the brainstorming or creative process and reduces it to an action step. We are very careful to preserve the sparks of innovation that were flying during the brainstorm. Look at it as moving from a moment of infinite opportunity into the realm of the possible. Prioritize the various ideas. Those most congruent with the overall objective become the components of the Project Plan. Overlay the Project Plan onto a timeline and assign action steps assigned to different team members. Remember to test the ideas against pre-established parameters you discussed at the outset of the brainstorm or creative process.

Here's the Project Plan concept in a real life example.

> ➤ We conducted brainstorm session to develop ideas for a new start-up company that focused on the conversion of apartments into affordable condominiums in smaller communities.

> ➤ The pre-ordained parameters included:

>> ◆ The ultimate sale price needed to be such that the monthly cost of principal, interest, taxes and insurance was less than the cost for

single family homes in the area, and only $75 to $100 more than monthly rent.

♦ Our business needed to generate a net profit of approximately $20,000 per unit.

➢ The brainstorm produced a number of ideas concerning what type of apartment properties we could acquire relative to age, location, price to purchase and physical condition. There were also ideas on how much we could spend on physical improvements. We discussed various loan programs including one that enabled working folks to purchase a condominium without having to come up with a down-payment. The team talked extensively about how to identify apartment properties that could be purchased for this conversion concept.

➢ After the brainstorm, we prioritized the ideas and a Project Plan was developed. Basic elements of the plan included:

♦ Target small Midwestern communities based upon size, demographics and population trends.

♦ Research the price of single family homes in each target market as well as to determine the range of rental rates.

♦ Call Realtors in the target communities to enlist their assistance in identifying and acquiring small apartment properties.

♦ Write to the owners of such properties in an attempt to begin a dialogue leading to purchase.

♦ Meet with the company offering the no-money-down loan program.

♦ We incorporated these steps into a timeline.

➤ A couple of team members then moved forward to implement the Project Plan. They made hundreds of phone calls and wrote countless offer letters to apartment owners in the target markets.

➤ After approximately ten months, we decided to shelve the concept. Our timing was off. We had anticipated a slowdown in the housing market and thought that apartment owners might be in a selling mood. Unfortunately the prices they wanted rivaled the prices of apartment properties in larger cities – except that the rents weren't anywhere close to being comparable. We were unable to find any apartment properties that we could acquire at a price that fit our financial model. About six months later, the housing market slowdown that we had anticipated became more apparent. Eventually we will take our concept and implement it when the price to purchase an apartment property finally matches our parameters.

There is a lot to take away from this example. The brainstorming process worked just like it was supposed to. We created the Project Plan and implemented the action steps as designed. And, we were smart enough to understand that until the anticipated slowdown became more pronounced, we might as well sit on the sidelines. But no one considers what we did to be a failure. It simply was an experiment that needs more time and tweaking before it will eventually succeed.

Channeling creativity into action can be a valuable cornerstone for an organization. Remember that the process must be positive and encouraging. Invite participants to problem-solve and to make mistakes without fear of consequences. If the environment is not positive and there is any aspect of fear, then the creative ideas will remain just that – ideas.

Outpacing Your Organization

The quintessential entrepreneur is a classic "fire starter." In other words, we have a million ideas and boundless energy. This combination is as combustible as pure oxygen and a tiny spark. What happens next is predictable. A raging inferno of creativity envelops the entire organization and the entrepreneur can't understand why everyone isn't caught up in his or her level of enthusiasm. This is where the "**keep-up**" factor enters the picture.

Several years ago we spent a small fortune on technology for our various companies. I studied the trends in technology and saw a multitude of creative applications for our businesses. We developed a loose plan for acquiring and implementing hardware and software applications with an eye toward enhanced productivity and providing better service for our clients. Early on the various members of our team were excited and quite proud that their company was investing in cutting edge technology. Our sales force bragged about their new tools. But as time passed, excitement gave way to bewilderment. Did I notice? No, I was too caught up in the euphoria of putting all of my ideas into action.

Eventually I looked over my shoulder and saw that no one was there. Up to that point, I hadn't understood why members of the team weren't fully utilizing all of the wonderful new resources. I couldn't fathom why people were resisting my newest technology initiatives. Then I realized that the ideas and the implementation had outpaced my organization. My teammates simply couldn't keep up with what they perceived to be a relentless technology onslaught.

I had created total chaos. Controlled chaos can be a good thing. Uncontrolled chaos is generally not. We had launched far too many technology applications. While we had provided adequate training we had not explained the overall vision in any coherent sort of way. Our people could understand a one or two dimensional strategy, but I had exploded this into an intricate multi-dimensional approach. What should I have done differently to harness the creative process in a sustained and beneficial manner? How could we have minimized the "keep-up" factor?

1. **Develop** – For starters, we should have developed a much more comprehensive strategy at the outset. I was certain that the technology

would improve productivity and provide better service to our clients. But that was far too broad of an objective.

2. **Collaborate** – A more collaborative strategy development process would have helped immensely. There were a few key people on board, but I wanted to move quickly and decisively. As a result, a number of my colleagues perceived (and maybe rightfully so) that I didn't value their input. I should have challenged the senior managers to work with me through the brainstorming process and allowed for the collaboration to drive our implementation. With greater participation the senior managers would have known the absorptive capacity of their teams. They could have helped stage the implementation in such a way as to minimize the "keep-up" factor.

3. **Buy-In** – Without buy-in from all corners of an organization, the best-intentioned concepts will not succeed to their full potential. We didn't realize the full range of benefits because we had only limited buy-in. Had senior managers and other key team members been selling the benefits we could have achieved a much greater acceptance of our creative ideas.

4. **Analyze** – Periodically it's smart to take a breather to absorb what has been implemented. This is a tough one for most entrepreneurs. We want to keep charging ahead. We should have factored in a period of months where no new technology initiatives were launched. We should have spent that time looking at what we had put into place and determining what was not working and how to tweak.

5. **Measure** – We really had no metrics to understand the effectiveness of our implementation. We should have had a series of metrics for every new technology application that we implemented should have to tell us if it was meeting our pre-established objectives. In other words, if a $10,000 software package was supposed to improve the productivity of our Marketing Department. Would we produce more sales brochures? How many more per day? Would we outsource less of the production process? How much would this save us?

Channeling creativity into action is important, but just as important is not outpacing your organization with your creativity. An entrepreneur must rely upon collaborative creativity. If he or she doesn't, it is easy to get carried away with the passion and energy derived from the process and fails to consider the impact on one's organization.

Action Summary

Creativity is a way to express your passion. And passion allows you to see in color. As entrepreneurs we strive for a life filled with rich and vibrant experiences. A great many of them come through the creative process. To realize the power of creativity, consider the following:

1. Stimulate creativity in a multitude of different ways.

    A. Read everything you can get your hands on. Be a sponge for information.

    B. Become a serial surfer of the Internet. Learn everything you can about the world around you.

    C. Find "thinking time" as often as possible. Take a long drive; sit for several hours on a sea shore or hike up to a mountain cabin. Do so for the specific purpose of encouraging your mind to generate new ideas.

    D. Listen to music.

    E. Work on puzzles – word searches, crossword puzzles, jigsaw puzzles and Sudoku.

2. Regularly organize and facilitate brainstorm sessions with your colleagues. Make sure to establish the overall objective of each brainstorm. Follow the rules of the brainstorming process and encourage partici-

pants to feed off of other people's ideas. Remember, that nothing is too wacky in a brainstorm session.

3.   Channel creativity into action. Prioritize your ideas. Effect a **"linear translation"** of those ideas into a Project Plan, complete with timeline and assignments. Look at it as moving from a moment of infinite opportunity into the realm of the possible.

4.   Don't outpace your organization with your ideas. Bring others into the creative process to develop the ideas further. You will need them to help you with the buy-in from the rest of your team. Push and challenge people, but don't get too far ahead of them or you'll encounter the **"keep-up"** factor. If this happens you won't realize the full benefit of your creativity.

Imagination is more important than knowledge.
~ **Albert Einstein**

CHAPTER 6

BE DIFFERENT

March to your own tune, but do so with a purpose.

I attended college during the early to mid-1970s. That was quite a time in our nation's history. Society was in upheaval with protests against the war in Vietnam; an explosion of drug use; free love; acid rock music, and the overall emergence of a counter-culture. A number of my classmates wore grungy (and sometimes, smelly) clothing, long hair, beards and beads. I wasn't interested in any of this. My hair wasn't long; I didn't grow a mustache or beard; I didn't ever use drugs of any sort; I didn't participate in sit-ins or protest marches, and I wore a coat and tie to class. There was never any feeling that I was better than anyone else. But even at the age of 18, I had a need to differentiate myself. This was all about being different with a purpose. By dressing, acting and looking different than my peers I said to my professors that I was a serious student. And they treated me as such, spending extra time answering my questions and helping me learn things that weren't in the text books.

Life in the 60s and 70s was a real paradox. Members of my generation were constantly chanting a doctrine of non-conformance and instead ended up conforming to a stereotype that they created for themselves. My generation preached individualism, yet many of my peers followed the herd in countless ways. I'll never forget the "streaking" craze that swept college campuses about this time. One bitterly cold morning while walking across campus to class I witnessed a young man (it was obvious) clad only in a stocking cap pulled down over his face and tennis shoes, jogging along the sidewalk. Another time, while sitting in class the door burst open and a completely naked male student ran in and around the desks and back out the door. The instructor stopped in mid-sentence, folded his arms and waited for the spectacle to end, then resumed his lecture as if nothing had ever happened. Incidents of these sorts finally led to a mass-student streak across campus one evening. There were estimates of a few hundred to a couple of thousand students participating in this "extracurricular activity." Talk about anti-individualism and conformity!

There are many reasons to be different with a purpose. Let's explore a few of them.

Morality and Integrity

Sometimes it's necessary to be different to preserve our sense of morality and integrity. As children and teens our social interaction was intertwined with a constant temptation to succumb to peer pressure. It takes real strength of character to be a contrarian in a world of conventional wisdom and to stick with your own moral principles.

As an entrepreneur the peer pressure can be intense. During the course of my career, I've known a number of high-flying commercial real estate magnates. I looked at what they were doing and wondered why I wasn't doing as well as they were. Many an employee and broker pointed to these individuals and their firms and asked, "Why can't you emulate them?" But over the years I watched as a number of these individuals fell from grace. One developer went to jail for creating fictitious leases that ultimately defrauded his lenders. Another firm saw two of its namesake principals go to prison for similar fraudulent schemes. Still another high-profile company went out of business and one of its principals had his real estate license revoked. My partners and I were different with a purpose. While the profits might have been greater in the short run by cutting corners, we plodded along, doing business and maintaining our integrity.

In Pursuit of Happiness

Would you rather be a miserable member of the in-crowd, or would you rather march to a different tune and be happy? The answer seems so simple. Yet many people complain about their miserable existence? It's not as easy as it looks.

I am different with a purpose because I choose to be happy. My parents instilled within me the belief that my happiness was within me and not with anyone else. I am completely and totally happy with my life. I've never felt the need to have the fanciest toys, live in the biggest house or chase after a little white ball for 6,500 yards. When I was in junior high school my parents decided to take up golf. They dragged me along to a public course that was in a river bottom and I swear that the air had not circulated there for over 100 years. The fairways were lined with cottonwood trees where the fuzz rained down and stuck to my sweaty arms, legs and neck. Simultaneously the mosquitoes would begin their synchronized dive bombing routine. They seemed to be attracted like a magnet to hot, sweaty cottonwood fuzz-covered skin. Meanwhile my parents were blithely and happily swinging away. Dad would top the ball and it would skitter along for 30 or 40 feet while Mom would whiff two or three shots before hitting it straight up in the air only to have it fall at her feet. They would shoot 90 or 100 on a good day – a respectable score for many a golfer – except that this was their score on NINE HOLES! As a result my ruination for the game of golf occurred about the time I started to shave.

I've been told that golf is a businessman's game and by the looks of it this premise is probably true. A lot of business deals are made on the golf course and undoubtedly I've missed making some of those deals. Still, I don't play golf because I don't want to. I am perfectly happy doing my own thing and isn't that the point in life? I don't do things that go against my grain. I don't pressure myself to conform or fit in.

Simply put, I don't do the things that don't give me pleasure if no one else is hurt in the process. I wear a coat and tie to my church every Sunday. Very few men in our congregation do so. I do it because it makes me feel right inside to do so. My motivations are pure. And, I'm different with a purpose.

To Achieve and Succeed

As an entrepreneur you must differentiate your product or service in order to win the sale. In some instances you must even differentiate yourself and/ or your team above and beyond your product or service. A lot of deals are done on the sheer power of the presentation or personality of the presenter. Thus, we spend our business lives looking for good and positive ways to be different.

In the early days of my commercial real estate career, our company took great pride in collecting extensive data that was unparalleled by any other firm in the Midwest. We invested significant sums of money to develop and maintain a database containing sale comparables, building facts, rental rates and a massive amount of other information. We published market reports for distribution to clients and prospective clients. The media often asked us for comments on market conditions and other aspects of our industry. Many of our competitors could not afford to produce the volumes of information that we could and for many years we were "king of the mountain."

Beginning in the mid-1990s, merely possessing information wasn't enough. Information was becoming a commodity. New companies specialized in collecting and selling data. Soon, everyone had access to the same data. We realized the need to change as this trend emerged and we focused on creating value with the information that we'd been collecting. Our team was constantly challenged to transform information into knowledge.

What exactly is involved with the transformation of information into knowledge? It's all about using distilled data to provide solutions to a myriad of issues and problems. The process of transforming information into knowledge starts with the premise that information unto itself is inert. If you don't do something with it, it is of no value. Now here's the big aha! At first, we followed conventional wisdom, trying to determine how the available data was relevant to a particular challenge. But that linear approach was limiting. So we took the information and looked for how we could use it to solve **any** problem. Problem-solving became three dimensional. We were always looking at every shred of information with an eye toward what problem it might be able to solve – not just the problem or issue needing immediate attention. In doing so, we expanded our thinking exponentially. Today, the ultimate way to differentiate taking one additional step: wrapping knowledge with experience to produce wisdom. What a way to differentiate!

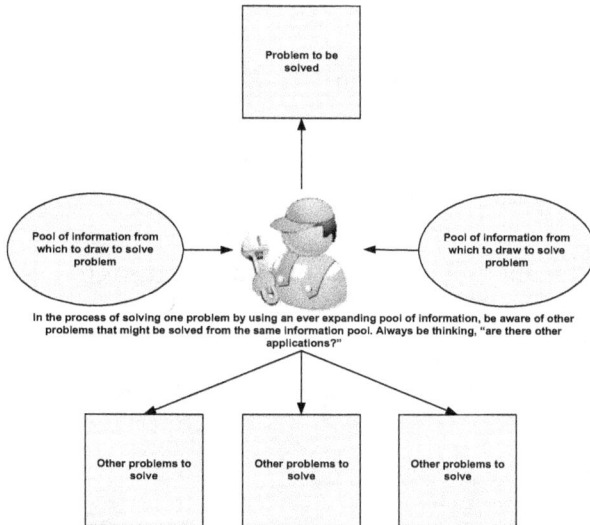

Figure 1
Problem Solving[x10]

How Are Entrepreneurs Different?

Who am I? As an entrepreneur how am I different from the rest of society?

1. I'm not afraid of big risks.

2. I will never be a victim and am responsible for my own choices and actions.

3. I have a high level of self-confidence and self-esteem.

4. I must always be challenged.

5. I am assertive while being outgoing. I am not self-conscious.

6. I couldn't survive in a big bureaucratic corporate environment.

7. I am a high-control person.

8. I'm constantly thinking about new business ideas and am not afraid to start a new business.

9. I can sell anything and am always trying to persuade people to see things my way.

10. I'm a natural leader but I'm not necessarily a manager.

11. I intuitively understand what customers want.

12. I'm tough when I get punched in the gut and will always get up and keep fighting.

13. I don't dwell on success or failure.

14. I'm about more than just money.

15. I will always be a rosy optimist.

16. I believe that competition makes me better.

17. I thrive on change.

18. I have boundless energy.

19. I need to be busy all the time.

20. I'll work long and hard but smart, to reach my goals.

21. I can handle high levels of stress.

22. I love solving complex problems.

23. I'm a big picture guy (or girl) – a true strategic thinker.

24. Imagination, creativity and innovation are my bywords.

Action Summary

1. Be different with a purpose because you choose to be happy.

2. Differentiate your product or service in order to win the sale. In some instances you must even differentiate yourself and/or your team above and beyond your product or service.

3. Don't be different just to be different.

4. Study and emulate the traits and tendencies of successful entrepreneurs.

> *If a man does not keep pace with his companions, perhaps it is because he hears a different drummer. Let him step to the music which he hears, however measured or far away.*
> ~ **Henry David Thoreau**

CHAPTER 7

RISK

Don't take risk . . . manage risk.

Most people understand the Risk/Reward equation. In theory, the more you risk the greater the reward. I'm an entrepreneur who absolutely refuses to take risks. The operative word here is "take." To "take" suggests that one simply <u>accepts</u> a particular risk. That doesn't work for me. I want the deck stacked in my favor. Not only that, I want to know every card in the deck and exactly how the cards are ordered. I want to aggressively and proactively manipulate risk. I want to ***manage*** risk.

Opportunities to Fail Exercise

I discovered what I call, the Opportunities to Fail Exercise quite accidentally – after I accidentally lost money in one of my ventures. For years I had been told that I looked at everything through rose-colored glasses. I chalked it up to my generally being a positive person. Instead, I was being naïve and unrealistic with my expectations. I was involved in the development and construction of a number of apartment properties in the mid-to-late 1990s involving low-income housing tax credits. Unfortunately, several of these properties were not successful. My partners and I ended up writing checks out of our own pockets to keep these projects financially viable. Had we undertaken an Opportunities to Fail Exercise before pursuing them, we never would have built some of the apartment complexes.

The Opportunities to Fail Exercise starts with an idea and a brainstorm session. I like to pull the entire team together and spend a couple of hours identifying every conceivable way the idea could fail. Using the development of affordable apartments as an example, the following might be some of the possible ways a project could go haywire.

1. Construction costs are significantly higher than projected.

2. The construction timeframe is significantly longer than projected.

3. The lease-up of the apartments takes significantly longer than expected.

4. Actual rental rates are lower than anticipated.

5. Operating expenses are higher than proposed.

6. A major employer shuts its doors causing higher sustained vacancy than projected.

An intense brainstorm may in fact identify 25, 50 or even 100 Opportunities to Fail. Don't get caught up trying to solve the issues during this brainstorm. The entire focus should be only upon cataloging the possible challenges. Also don't worry about whether a particular potential point of failure seems too far-fetched or obscure – identify every possibility. Then let the list sit for a few days. Share it with all members of the team and allow anyone to add to the list.

Risk Mitigation

Schedule a second brainstorm session with the team for the purpose of mitigating each of the Opportunities to Fail on the list. Some challenges will be easy to solve. Others may yield more uncertain results. Let's go back to the affordable apartment development scenario.

1. Construction costs are significantly higher than projected.

    A. Mitigation – Project does not proceed unless a contractor has provided a firm-bid price that does not exceed projections.

2. The construction timeframe is significantly longer than projected.

    A. Mitigation – The construction contract will contain substantial monetary penalties for delays in completion.

3. The lease-up of the apartments takes significantly longer than expected.

    A. Mitigation – Do not proceed with the project unless a comprehensive independent market study clearly demonstrates that the market is deep enough to quickly absorb the proposed project's units at the designated price points.

    B. Mitigation – Start the lease-up at the same time that construction starts.

4. Actual rents are lower than anticipated.

    A. Mitigation – Do not proceed unless a comprehensive independent market study clearly demonstrates that the market will easily accept the proposed rental rates.

5. Operating expenses are higher than proposed.

    A. Mitigation – Have an expert property manger create a month-by-month line item budget for the first three years of operation. Use this instead of a general summary category pro-forma prepared by a member of the development staff.

6. A major employer shuts its doors causing higher sustained vacancy than projected.

    A. Mitigation – Do not proceed unless a comprehensive independent market study clearly demonstrates that the project can succeed in spite of the loss of a major employer.

After completing the Opportunities to Fail Exercise you are ready to decide whether or not to proceed with implementing your idea. I look at how well the various risks can be mitigated and make my decision accordingly. If any of the "biggies" are in doubt, then I abandon or delay the idea. But I no longer worry about flushing a potential deal if it doesn't survive the Opportunities to Fail Exercise. I just immediately launch into examining the next idea.

Margin of Safety

Almost everyone has heard the legendary Warren Buffet talk about a concept introduced by his mentor, Benjamin Graham. Three simple words – Margin of Safety – should become the guiding light for every entrepreneur. You can't manage risk without it. Graham's technical definition of Margin of Safety stipulates that when a company is available on the market at a price that is at a discount to its intrinsic value then a margin of safety exists, which makes it suitable for investment. Investopedia further defines intrinsic value as "the actual value of a company or an asset based on an underlying perception of its true value including all aspects of the business, in terms of both tangible and intangible factors. This value may or may not be the same as the current market value."

Margin of Safety is like having a couple of aces hidden up my sleeve. From an entrepreneurial perspective, creating Margin of Safety is the next logical progression after passing the Opportunities to Fail Exercise.

In our affordable apartment development example how might we create Margin of Safety?

1. Find enough sources of funds so there are surplus funds left over. In addition to securing a traditional loan on the property along with the equity from the investors we will look for money from additional parties – perhaps grant funding is available from the state for incorporating energy conservation methods into the project. Or maybe federal and state historic tax credits can be included if we're renovating an historic structure.

2. We take the surplus funds and create cash reserves. Perhaps we'll set extra money aside just in case we need to enhance our marketing efforts to ensure 100% occupancy when we open the project. Maybe we'll establish an operating reserve just in case the real estate taxes are higher than anticipated and we have to go to court to get them lowered. Rather than perfectly match our sources and uses of funds (which is what I did earlier in my career) we over-source our financial model in a prudent way to improve our odds of success.

3. Instead of just leasing our project to the point of 100% occupancy and stopping there, we'll continue our marketing efforts and build a waiting list. This is a great way to achieve better-than-projected occupancy rates but it also makes our apartment property seem to be in greater demand. And we all know the emotional drive that is generated when demand exceeds supply.

The Margin of Safety concept requires a whole new mindset. No longer do we think about perfectly aligning our idea in symmetrical fashion – i.e. having it turn out in reality exactly how we modeled it. Margin of Safety pushes into an asymmetrical space. An idea that is perfectly shaped, perfectly symmetrical, has no room for error. Let's extend this metaphor to a more concrete illustration. Draw a perfect square and pretend like it's the ultimate manifestation of an idea. Then draw an additional smaller square and attach it to the upper left hand side of the larger square. The smaller square represents Margin of Safety.

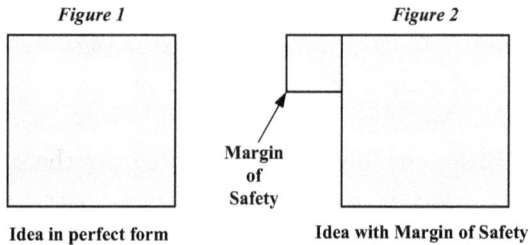

Figure 1

Idea in perfect form

Figure 2

**Margin
of
Safety**

Idea with Margin of Safety

I know the square in Figure 2 no longer looks pretty with the Margin of Safety hanging onto it. But guess what? Suppose during the implementation of the idea the square turns out looking like this:

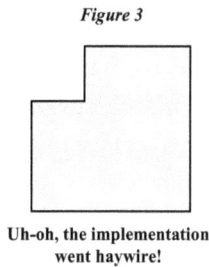

Figure 3

**Uh-oh, the implementation
went haywire!**

Yep, you figured it out. The Margin of Safety restores the end result to something more like you envisioned in the beginning.

Figure 4

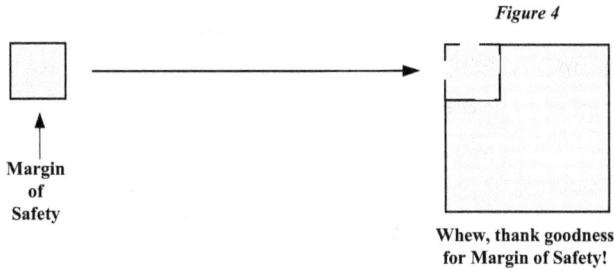

Margin
of
Safety

Whew, thank goodness
for Margin of Safety!

In Chapter 3, I mentioned that I whipped my fear of flying and became a pilot. The airplane that I purchased was for recreational purposes. Several mechanics told me that it was in great physical condition. But I wanted more assurance – after all, the mechanics were always on the ground. And I knew with total certainty that I always wanted to be in a situation where I was on the ground wishing I was flying, than flying and wishing I was on the ground! So I created several Margins of Safety. I took the operating manual for the plane and created my own specific pre-flight checklist. I took a lot of ribbing from the other pilots about my multi-page laminated checklist and the meticulous manner in which I pre-flighted the plane. But I didn't care. The Margin of Safety I had created was far more important to me than enduring a bit of good-natured teasing.

Exploiting the Opportunity

After we've mitigated all our Opportunities to Fail and created our Margin of Safety, we're ready to Exploit the Opportunity.

A shrewd and crafty general develops a battle plan using this layered approach. He looks for all of the weaknesses in his ideas, and then shores them up so they are no longer weaknesses. Then he makes sure he has something extra that will tip the battle in his favor. But he doesn't stop there. He wants to march on to victory by defeating the enemy and capturing the territory it occupies. General Daniel Morgan did exactly this during the Battle of the Cowpens on January 17, 1781, during the American Revolution. General Ulysses S. Grant had a similar strategy during the Battle of Vicksburg during the Civil War.

Once again let's turn to the example of our affordable apartment development. We've undertaken the Opportunities to Fail Exercise and successfully mitigated each and every challenge. We've identified several possible Margins of Safety through additional sources of funds that will be used for various reserves, as well as marketing and leasing to create a waiting list. But before we begin there's something more we can do to Exploit the Opportunity and actually make this project far better than ever imagined.

Here's an example. We were looking for ways to make our projects safer as an investment and more profitable. After much research we have discovered that there was a need for a small medical clinic in the immediate area. We made contact with the state university's medical school. The university was willing to lease, staff and operate a medical clinic on a long-term basis if we were willing to provide the facility. Our initial plans called for a large clubhouse on our property. With some minor modification, we could have a clubhouse for our residents to use AND a facility for the medical clinic. We had the same apartment community we had originally planned but we now had significantly more income generated by the rent paid by the medical clinic. And our residents could receive basic health care services on premise. The waiting list for this property grew and existing residents didn't want to move because of this extra benefit. Now that is really Exploiting the Opportunity!

Risk Simulation and Sensitivity

The quantification of risk is helpful in understanding how to manage it. One technique that I do find invaluable is creating a sensitivity analysis. I look at different combinations of variables to see what the downside and upside range might be. For our affordable apartment development the sensitivity variables might look like this:

Variable	Baseline	Low	High
Construction Costs	$4,000,000	$3,750,000	$4,500,000
Lease-Up Period	180-days	90-days	270-days
Initial Rental Rates	$450	$425	$475
Annual Rent Increase Factor	2.0%	1.0%	3.0%
Initial Operating Expenses/ Unit	$3,750	$3,500	$4,000
Annual Operating Expense Increase Factor	2.5%	2.0%	3.0%
Stabilized Occupancy	92.5%	90.0%	95.0%

To get the sensitivity range, we target a baseline amount and then determine the absolute lowest and highest on either side of the baseline. We then construct a spreadsheet to create a sensitivity analysis that solves for the greatest downside number and the greatest upside number. That "number" might be the overall profit on the project development; it might be annual net distributable cash, or both.

If the downside number is truly out of balance with the upside number then you must consider whether to deploy your resources for such a low yielding investment. For example, let's say that the affordable apartment development that we have continually referenced has a baseline developer fee of $500,000. The lowest fee the developer would receive is $325,000 and the most is $600,000. This represents a fairly tight range in the overall sensitivity calculus and we would probably proceed as planned. However, suppose the baseline is a $500,000 fee, the downside is a $1.2 million loss (meaning that we have to come out of pocket to finish the project) and the upside fee is $600,000. We would have to seriously consider whether or not to proceed with a project that has such a huge downside potential. Remember that the Opportunities to Fail Exercise, risk mitigation and Margin of Safety are active steps that we take to manage risk. Their success is not an absolute. Yes I'm highly confident in this process but remember how I want to stack the deck in my favor. I always want my pipeline of ideas to be so full that I'm always able to make choices between ideas and can discard those where the downside potential is too great.

The Final Equation

Managing risk is an "equational process." It is best demonstrated by the diagram below.

Figure 5

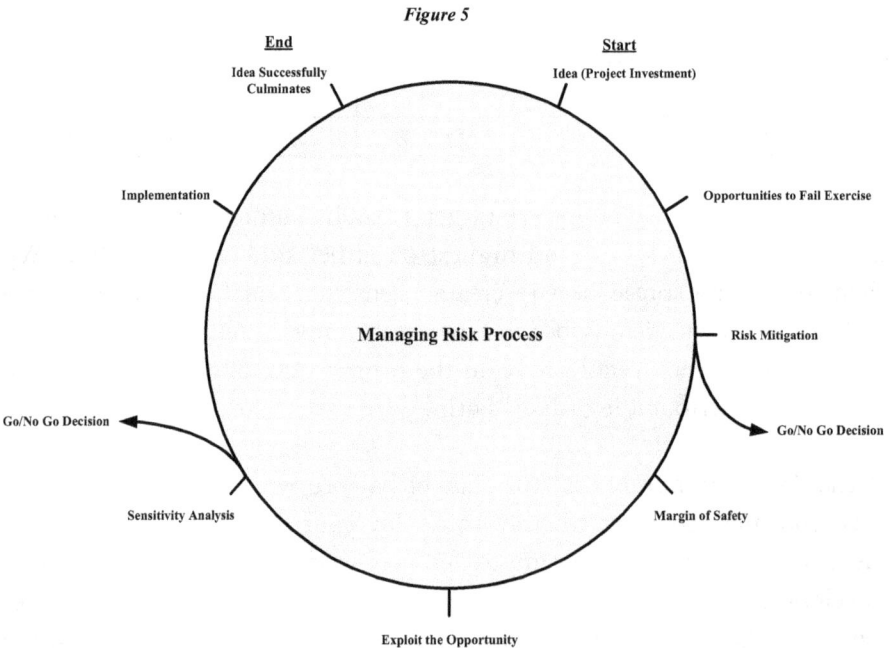

| End | Start |

Idea Successfully Culminates — Idea (Project Investment)

Implementation — Opportunities to Fail Exercise

Managing Risk Process — Risk Mitigation

Go/No Go Decision — Go/No Go Decision

Sensitivity Analysis — Margin of Safety

Exploit the Opportunity

The equational aspect of the process comes in several of the steps including Risk Mitigation, Margin of Safety, Exploiting the Opportunity and the Sensitivity Analysis.

As an entrepreneur I never want to "take" a risk. I only want to manage risk. Understanding the concept of Risk/Reward is only the first baby step toward the true management of risk.

Action Summary:

1. Schedule a brainstorming exercise with your team to identify all of the Opportunities to Fail. Record every conceivable way your idea (project, investment) could turn upside down.

2. Hold a second brainstorming session to develop a Risk Mitigation strategy for every potential point of failure.

3. If you can't successfully figure out how you are going to neutralize all of the risks, scrap the idea and analyze the next idea in the same way.

4. If you can successfully mitigate all of the significant risks, then look for Margins of Safety that can further protect you from the potential of failure.

5. Now think big. Try and see what can be done to tweak your idea (without adding risk). What additional opportunities can you exploit?

6. Perform a Sensitivity Analysis to explore the upside and downside potential around a baseline projection.

7. If the downside potential is too great, scrap the idea and move on to the next one.

8. If the downside potential is reasonable then move forward to implement your idea. And, good luck!

> *There is no security on this earth. Only opportunity.*
> ~ **General Douglas MacArthur**

CHAPTER 8

RELATIONSHIPS

The success of a career can be measured in the number of lasting relationships that have been collected and nurtured.

Relationships are an entrepreneur's lifeblood. From a business perspective, I want to have real and meaningful relationships that are so strong and committed that my competitors can't pry them loose.

Know People

The first step in forming relationships is to ask questions and get to know people. You are looking for points of connection. How can you relate to this person and how can they relate to you? The process of gathering information and clues must become intuitive and second nature. If not, you come across as manipulative. A few of the things I like to learn about people include:

➢ Where did they grow up?

➢ What is their favorite job?

➤ What sort of family do they have? A spouse? Children? How many and how old?

➤ In what activities do their children participate?

➤ What are their hobbies?

➤ Does their spouse work and if so, where?

➤ What books do they read?

➤ What music do they listen to?

➤ Where do they go on vacation?

➤ What are their big picture hopes and dreams?

➤ What do they fear most?

These questions are about making a connection. What do you have in common with someone else? What sort of fascinating things has this person done in his or her life? Who do they know that you know?

You've probably heard the phrase "Six Degrees of Separation." Stanley Milgram, a Yale psychologist, confirmed the theory that everyone is no more than six "steps" away from every person on Earth, meaning that person A only needs a maximum of six people to connect to person B (supposing A and B don't know each other).

I have often experienced the Six Degrees of Separation. I had dinner once with a man from Detroit. One of our clients recommended that he call us. During a meeting I learned that an accountant acquaintance of ours had also recommended that he talk to us. Then I learned that we knew his ex-brother-in-law quite well. Throughout the course of the evening the world got a whole lot smaller as we discovered more mutual friends and acquaintances.

Common friends and acquaintances strengthen the connection between people. Having children similar in age, activities and challenges creates another common bond.

Knowing people requires you to become a people watcher. How does a person dress? Is he or she drawn to high fashion? How do they wear their hair? Are their shoes shined? Is there a sparkle in their eyes? How firm is their handshake? A handshake can speak volumes about someone. Firm but not crushing; warm hands but not clammy, and just the right length of time in the clasp.

How gracious is the person in a restaurant? Does he or she acknowledge the wait staff and say please and thank you? Does he or she gesture when speaking? Can you see tattoos? Does the person look you in the eye when speaking? Is this person easily distracted?

If you are in a person's workspace what do you see? Are there plaques and awards on the wall? Is there family? Is the person's desk neat and orderly or is it a mess? How is the seating arranged?

My office is an easy read. I have photos of my wife, daughters and grandson as well as a number of models of airplanes and some aviation art framed on the walls. I generally work with next to nothing on my desk and my credenza is clear (yes, I'm a neat freak). I've always wanted to hang some velvet nude paintings on my walls (the kind you buy in Tijuana) just to throw people off. But I stick with the airplanes.

Remember the focus is on the other person and not you. The surest way NOT to build a relationship is to make most of the conversation about you.

Building the Relationship

How do you decide to build a relationship? Just about everyone that I connect with is a potential relationship. The connection really determines if a relationship will develop.

I like to think of my relationships as friendships. Friendship elevates a relationship and adds a sense of duty. Our planet is filled with interesting people who have knowledge and experience that can enrich our lives. When I extend my hand in friendship it firmly cements that relationship with these wonderful people.

Relationships are about serving people. As you went through the "getting to know" process you learned a great deal about a person's likes, dislikes, wants and needs. You are well equipped to look for opportunities to meet the needs of the person with whom you are building a relationship. But meeting the needs of other people requires an investment of your time, talent, treasure and even your emotions.

A friend of mine is in the moving and storage business. He is one of the most warm-hearted people I've ever known. I always hear from him on my birthday and my wedding anniversary. If I'm sick he sends something to cheer me up. When we go to dinner he always wants to pick up the tab or buy me a drink. He treats all of his relationships the same way. He has never asked me for anything. Of course I've contracted with his company when we moved our businesses. And I always recommend him to people. But I find it very enlightening that in all the years I've known him he's never had his hand out for one single thing. He's all about serving his fellow man.

Think about the way you are building relationships. Do you see other people as potential "targets" to mine for business? Or do you see them as friends? If you aren't quite sure you are on the right track re-dedicate yourself to finding ways to serve the people with whom you have relationships. And do so with the purest of intentions. This means getting out of yourself. Revel in the success of others. I like to honor relationships that have received public recognition. When a nice article appears in a weekly business newspaper about a friend or acquaintance, I'll have it transferred onto a plaque for that person. I send a lot of personal handwritten notes to people. The old-fashioned handwritten note says something that a three or four sentence e-mail can't say. A well-placed personal phone call speaks so much louder than a text message or writing on someone's Facebook wall.

If I can introduce you to someone who may help your business, then I'm serving our relationship. If I can support your charitable cause in some way (financially or otherwise) then I'm serving our relationship. If I can be a shoulder to cry on when you're having a tough time, I'm serving our relationship. A number of years ago a reporter for a business publication sought me out with some frequency for quotes on various happenings in the commercial real estate industry. He was a great guy and one of the fairest and most professional reporters I ever met. One day he told me that he thought he might have a serious skin cancer. I listened to him and shared with him some of my personal beliefs, then invited him to call me day or night if he ever needed to talk. I'll never forget the late night call I received after he had been diagnosed with the disease. He was frightened and needed support. We talked about his fears, about his son and what he needed to do to fight the cancer. There were other phone calls in the ensuing days and weeks and he went into remission for a time. Throughout our friendship I learned how to be more empathetic. I marveled at how someone fighting for his life could be so courageous. His quiet strength was an inspiration for me. When he died a few years later I sat at his funeral and knew that I had done everything I could to serve our relationship.

You see, there's more than dollars and cents at stake here. People's <u>lives</u> are at stake and the way we serve our relationships can have a tremendous impact on their lives. If you can understand and believe this premise, the way you serve your relationships will change forever.

Is there any difference between real relationships and customer or client relationships? I tend to treat all of my relationships on a friendship level. I'll make darn sure we provide the best service possible and reach out to connect whenever I can. Above all I want to make certain the customer/client's needs are always being met. Perhaps the chemistry may be better if the client builds a relationship with someone else in my company. That's fabulous because there's a greater chance that a deeper relationship will develop and be served if such a connection is made.

The Benefits of Relationships

I know you've been waiting for this part of the chapter. You've been thinking, "I'm investing an awful lot of time, talent, treasure and maybe even some emotion into a relationship. But can't I get a little something out of all of this?" The simple answer is, yes you can. But stick with me a little longer.

One of our business units was a commercial leasing and brokerage operation. We had a large number of salespeople who leased and sold office buildings, shopping centers, industrial facilities and raw land. They all worked on a straight commission basis and had a fairly short-term mentality. For many years I tried to convince members of the sales team to take the time to build real relationships. They just wanted to do deals. I demonstrated how they would dramatically increase their income if they nurtured real relationships. They just wanted to do deals. I gave them a multitude of examples of how beneficial building real and lasting relationships had been to my partners and me. They just wanted to do deals. We only had a couple of sales agents dedicated to building relationships. They made the big money on a sustained basis. Most of our salespeople did not have the patience for real relationships. They didn't see the value of real relationships because all they wanted to do was chase the dollar for themselves. Many of them made decent money but they didn't realize their full potential.

The Law of Attraction applies abundantly to relationships. As children we learned the Golden Rule – do unto others as you would have them do unto you. When you start serving your relationships without ulterior motives, all sorts of good comes your way. Because you've subjugated your ego, you tap into an energy flow that allows you to receive new opportunities. Getting yourself out of the way often solves problems and opens new and wonderful.

I've built real relationships with people from whom I've never directly earned a nickel. But they have introduced me to other people who have done business with me and generated substantial sums of money for our businesses. I've served some relationships for more than 20 years before a pay day ever occurred. That was fine because I didn't seek out the relationship to make money. Investing time, talent, treasure and emotion in each relationship produces an energy flow that delivers good to you in so many different ways and from so many different sources. Maybe the good doesn't come from one relationship in the form of a check. Maybe it comes in the form of an inspiration. If you think one-dimensionally about your relationships – and that is solely about money – you won't realize all of your good. But if you think multi-dimensionally, your good will come in many different manifestations.

Real relationships will make you healthy, wealthy and wise. They feed your soul. At times you will be getting back far more than you're putting in. And it's OK. Always remember that it's about the opportunity to serve others. It's about doing what it takes to meet their needs. It's about getting yourself out of the way.

Partnership is an extension of a relationship. As an entrepreneur I love the idea of partnership as much as I like the concept of relationship. In a relationship I'm committed to serving another party and meeting his or her needs to the best of my ability. That doesn't necessarily mean that the other person has reciprocated the commitment. In a partnership both parties have a vested interest in each other's success and well-being.

I become practically giddy when I can convert a vendor-vendee relationship into a partnership. That means the vendor and I have an alignment of interest. We each want to help the other succeed and it's in our mutual best interest to do so. Here's a real life example.

Our property management group has built a relationship with an individual at a large pension fund advisory firm. He hired us to manage an apartment property for his firm. We serve the relationship faithfully and meet the needs of our client at every turn. However in his mind, we have a vendor (us)/vendee (him) relationship. We changed that dynamic when we found additional properties his firm can purchase. He is always looking for investment opportunities.

Now we're no longer just a property manager for a single property. We have become a pipeline for acquisitions. Not only do we continue managing the initial property but we also manage the properties that we assist our client in purchasing. AND, our client also retains us to manage other properties. He is committed to our success not just because we do a great job of managing his property but also because we supply him with new properties. We are committed to his success because he hires us to manage more of his properties. Our one-dimensional relationship has blossomed into a mutually beneficial partnership.

Look for ways to enhance a relationship so that it can become a partnership. This works in all types of relationships.

Action Summary

1. Strive to build real relationships – not convenience relationships.

2. Get to know people. Ask questions about them and look for clues that give you insight into their wants and needs.

3. Maintain the purity of your motives. If you are looking to manipulate people you will be unsuccessful in your quest.

4. Remember that the focus of a relationship is on the other party. Get yourself out of the way. Ultimately it's about serving the wants and needs of others.

5. To build real relationships you must invest time, talent, treasure and emotions.

6. Don't always look for a direct cause and effect with your relationships. Be open to the energy that flows and the good that comes your way when you serve the needs of others.

7. Convert your relationships to partnerships whenever possible. Aligning your interests in this manner brings with it a mutual commitment to help each other succeed.

I don't want to be just a voice on the phone. I have to get to know these guys face-to-face and develop a sincere relationship. That way, if we run into problems in a deal, it doesn't get adversarial. We trust each other and have the confidence we can work things out.
~ Wayne Huizenga

CHAPTER 9

LAUGH LIKE CRAZY

Laugh every chance you get . . . especially at yourself.

My life has been filled with laughing, chortling, snickering, giggling, snorting, cackling and sometimes tears-streaming, gasping-for-air hysterics. I can't imagine living any other way. So what does laughter have to do with being a successful entrepreneur? The physiology of laughter is quite fascinating. Helpguide.org says this about laughter:

> ➤ **Laughter lowers blood pressure** – People who laugh heartily on a regular basis have lower standing blood pressure than the average person. When people have a good laugh, initially the blood pressure increases, but then it decreases to levels below normal. Breathing then becomes deeper which sends oxygen enriched blood and nutrients throughout the body.

> ➤ **Humor changes our biochemical state** – Laughter decreases stress hormones and increases infection fighting antibodies. It increases our attentiveness, heart rate, and pulse.

> ➤ **Laughter protects the heart** – Laughter, along with an active sense of humor, may help protect you against a heart attack, according

to a study at the University of Maryland Medical Center. The study, which is the first to indicate that laughter may help prevent heart disease, found that people with heart disease were 40 percent less likely to laugh in a variety of situations compared to people of the same age without heart disease.

➤ **Laughter gives our bodies a good workout** – Laughter can be a great workout for your diaphragm, abdominal, respiratory, facial, leg, and back muscles. It massages abdominal organs, tones intestinal functioning, and strengthens the muscles that hold the abdominal organs in place. Laughter also can benefit digestion and absorption functioning as well. Hearty laughter can burn calories equivalent to several minutes on the rowing machine or the exercise bike.

➤ **Humor improves brain function and relieves stress** – Laughter stimulates both sides of the brain to enhance learning. It eases muscle tension and psychological stress, which keeps the brain alert and allows people to retain more information.

In addition to a favorable physical reaction in the body, laughter also helps to create a positive state of mind and reinforces positive energy. Here's an affirmation I use: "I live from a positive view of the world and celebrate life."

Figure 1

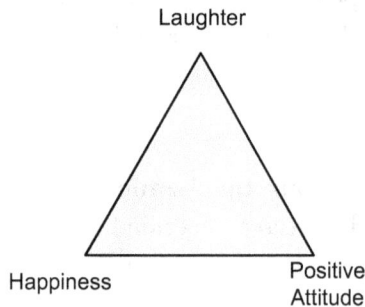

Laughter

Happiness   Positive Attitude

Laughter Builds Relationships

Laughter and humor can be extremely helpful in the relationship building process. Most people seem to be drawn to those who are funny, happy and laugh a lot.

Timing is everything when it comes to laughter and humor. You must size up the situation and the mood of the other people. If someone is looking particularly glum, find out (in a subtle way) what is wrong. Don't crack a joke or tease someone only to find out that his father had died. Yet there are other times when humor may be just the right remedy. The glum looks of several colleagues might be the result of losing a contract and a little could be all that's needed to get this group jump-started. Read the moment. Read the people. Be natural.

Laugh at Yourself

A good entrepreneur has no problem laughing at him or herself. When something goes wrong and you are the cause of it, the most constructive thing you can do is laugh and learn. That is, laugh at your own inattention or miscalculation and learn what to do next time so the mistake is not repeated.

For example I may use an absurd comparison to invoke my own (twisted) laughter. Let's say I just made a mistake that cost us $1,000. I might say to myself like, "Well at least it didn't cost us $1,001!" The little laugh that follows neutralizes the negative aspect of the moment and allows me to figure out what to do differently in the future. By the way, this process may take all of 30 seconds or less. It helps to develop a trigger that causes you to laugh at yourself. When you can make fun of yourself it humanizes you. If anyone previously perceived you as being aloof, your humor certainly destroys that image.

Having a bout with the "clumsies" as an adult can be turned into a great opportunity to make other people smile. A group of my partners and I, meet in my office every Monday for a working lunch. Recently I made the mistake of reaching for my salad while I putting on my reading glasses. I misjudged my reach and salad went flying all over me, the chair mat and the! Everyone started laughing and I was laughing the loudest. Now each Monday, I make a big production out of taking off my reading glasses before I reach for my salad. Everyone still gets a chuckle out of this.

Use Humor to Lighten Up

There is a longstanding belief that humor is a great way to start a speech. Causing laughter has a way of loosening up the audience. You've made a connection and people tend to pay attention more closely. You can almost feel the flow of positive energy when the first wave of laughter washes over the room. Using humor and laughter at the beginning of a speech or presentation helps you lighten up as well. If you are a bit nervous, a bit of levity can be the perfect tonic to put you at ease.

Humor and laughter can also be appropriate in tense situations – especially if for some reason you are the focal point of the situation. It can help defuse the tension being felt by others.

Practice Laughing

Practice laughter whenever possible. Go to comedy clubs, watch sitcoms (the really funny ones) and hilarious movies. Read the funny paper. Buy humorous calendars. Immerse yourself in joy, happiness and laughter whenever you can. You'll live longer, you'll enjoy life to a much greater extent and your relationships will be even better.

Share your laughter with others. Make it your daily mission to see that everyone you see has a smile or a laugh as a result of what you do and say.

Action Summary

1. Laughter produces many physical benefits. Laugh for your health.

2. Use laughter to build relationships. People like to be around other people who are happy.

3. Laugh at yourself especially when you goof. The bigger your flub-up the harder you should laugh. Then you'll be in the right frame of mind to learn what to do differently next time.

4. Use laughter and humor to loosen up an audience and yourself.

5. Practice laughing every chance you get. Happiness, joy and laughter should be part of who you are.

Laughter is an instant vacation.
~ **Milton Berle**

CHAPTER 10

GIVE IT AWAY

What you give will come back to you in amazing and wonderful ways.

Take the following survey and see where you rate.

1. I get more pleasure out of giving than receiving.

Yes ____   No ____

Pretty short survey, huh? This chapter is about how giving and tithing will make you a better entrepreneur. Long ago my wife and I made the decision to give away our treasure. We live comfortably and do not have to make sacrifices in order to accommodate our lifestyle. While we love our children we believe that they need to make their own way; and so they won't be getting a large inheritance after we're gone. Through a variety of estate planning techniques our children and grandchildren will receive substantial incomes; just not the principal amount itself. But we're not waiting until we die to do good things with our good fortune.

A number of years ago we started a scholarship program at our alma mater for young women and men who want to become teachers. Neither of us has ever taught school but we believe that teaching is so important to our society. We also have chosen to tithe more than 10% of our income to our church. We believe that the more money we put back into "circulation" through tithing and giving, the more good that will come back to us. And we are living proof of this principle.

Tithing

Simply put, tithing means giving 10% of your income to the source that feeds your soul. In my case, that source is my church. I actually created a partnership with my church. My minister and I have breakfast or lunch once a quarter to talk about our partnership and review our progress. She and her team support me in different ways. For example, my creative energy increases exponentially during and after a church service. The more I learn from church teachings, the healthier my interaction with others and my relationships are stronger and more meaningful. Without question my soul is more complete and my spirit is move alive as a result of "plugging in" to the consciousness that is provided through my church.

The other side of our partnership involves tithing and giving. In addition to tithing my wife and I both volunteer to make a contribution of our time and talent. There is no pledge requirement at our church. I'm happy to share my income figures with my minister and even happier to write my checks each week. I'm giving from my heart and I'm receiving such an abundance of food for my soul.

Where did the 10% factor originate? Actually there is a story in the Bible (Genesis 14:18-20) that started it all. But before I share the story let me make this statement. I am not advocating any religion at all in this book. This biblical story is spiritual, not religious.

And Melchizedek king of Salem brought out bread and wine. (He was priest of God Most High.) And he blessed him and said, "Blessed be Abram by God Most High, possessor of heaven and earth; and blessed be God Most High, who has delivered your enemies into your hand!" And Abram gave him a tenth of everything.

How do we know whether or not tithing 10% actually comes back to us through additional prosperity? In my life, it has worked so many times that it's actually become second nature. Once when I was scratching my head about how to bridge a short-term financial gap it suddenly occurred to me that a portion of a large developer's fee was still owed to us on a particular property. This could have been paid at any time over the prior couple of years but somehow it had "dropped off the radar screen." Why it hit me at that precise moment I attribute to the Law of Attraction – of which tithing is a part.

In another instance I was considering making a specific investment. To do so, I would have needed to liquidate another investment that wasn't quite performing to my expectations. Then out-of-the-blue a property sale I'd been working on came together. The fee provided the capital I needed to make the new investment. And wouldn't you know it, the investment that I had planned to liquidate caught fire and I ended up with a "two-fer." Again, I believe that this prosperity came to me because my tithing and the Law of Attraction.

Develop a Strategy

Here's a recommendation that may resonate with you. Develop a strategy for your giving. Start with a Vision. My wife and I have a very simple Vision for "giving it away." Here it is.

We want to provide our time, talent and treasure to our church, to our university and to future and current teachers in our state while we are alive and after we are gone. We want the financial component of this support to equal at least $X.

Let's break this down.

1. We want to give away our financial resources both while we're alive and after we depart this mortal plane.

2. We want to support our church.

3. We want to support various programs at the university that launched our careers.

4. We want to provide support to young people in our state who wish to teach school.

5. We want to provide support to existing teachers in our state to help them afford to remain in the profession.

6. Finally we've established a minimum dollar figure that we want to give away during and after our lives.

My quest in my business life is in part to make a lot of money. This is an objective shared by most entrepreneurs. But I'm motivated to create significant wealth so that I can build toward the minimum dollar amount that we have identified in our vision.

So the Vision is clear. Now, how do we make it happen? The next step is to develop a strategy that delivers the Vision. Our strategy is comprised of the following:

1. Tithe at least 10% of our income to our church while we are alive.

2. Fund an endowment for our church that will provide the same 10% income equivalency after we die.

3. Identify programs at our university that we wish to support during our lifetime. This may take the form of both expendable gifts as well as endowments as we see fit.

4. Provide expendable funds for our teacher's scholarship program through our university.

5. Fund an endowment for our university teacher's scholarship program that will allow for it to be continued and potentially expanded after we are gone.

6. Provide expendable funds for a new teacher's support program that will offer supplemental income stipends to deserving teachers in our state. These teachers will be required to offer their teaching services outside of their normal classrooms to help meet the needs of their community.

7. Fund an endowment for the supplemental income stipends that are paid to existing teachers, allowing the program to continue in perpetuity.

8. Offer our time and our talent to the various programs described in our Vision.

As you can see, we have a Vision and we have a Strategy for our philosophy of "giving it away." We've chosen the recipients based upon our belief system and our values. I have a well-defined purpose for continuing to pursue my business ventures in order to make a lot of money. And our Vision and Strategy helps us concentrate and direct our funding efforts to achieve the maximum benefits for the designated recipients.

You may be thinking, "Does this really apply to me? I don't really have much in the way of financial resources at this point in my life." Get rid of such thoughts right now. You can start tithing at any stage of your life. You simply give 10% of your income – whatever it may be – to the source that feeds your soul. Part of the purpose in visioning and creating a strategy is to set your own aspirations and expectations. If you are reading this book you are well on your way to becoming a highly successful entrepreneur, so setting goals should be an easy thing for you to do.

Tools for Giving it Away

There are many tools that can help you achieve your vision. First, hire an estate planning attorney to help you select the best tools to deliver maximum value to the beneficiaries of your largesse.

1. Irrevocable Life Insurance Trusts (ILIT) – My wife and I each have an ILIT. The ILITs own our life insurance policies. I'm a big believer in buying life insurance as early in life as possible. I have purchased as much as I could afford and added policies as I've gotten older. Initially this was done to provide a nest egg to build income for my family should I die. I maintain the policies as a source of funds that builds toward the minimum "give away" amount contained in our Vision.

2. Charitable Remainder Trust (CRT) – With a CRT you are giving away some of your assets at the time the trust is formed. Let's say that your Vision calls for you to make one or more gifts to your alma mater. You could make the gift now and receive a tax deduction for your donation. The university (or more likely its foundation or endowment association) will invest the funds you gave and pay you (and maybe your spouse after you are gone) the income that is generated. You need to understand that you've permanently and irretrievably given away this money (or real estate, securities – whatever you might have chosen to give). You have no further control over these funds. Further, your university will receive no benefit from your gift until you die because the corpus must be invested (rather than expended) and the income comes to you and not the university. Still the CRT is an important tool and one of several that you might wish to utilize to deliver your Vision.

3. Family Foundation – We established a family foundation because we wanted a repository for all of our investment and estate planning vehicles. Our foundation allows us to very precisely direct our charitable funding desires. Here's an example of how this might apply. Part of our Vision is to provide funding for existing teachers who are willing to teach within their communities outside of their regular classrooms. While we're alive we'll provide funding for this project directly. We

will also have influence over the creation and administration of the program. We expect to create a 501(c)3 tax-exempt entity to receive and disburse funds, but it my not be capable of handling an endowment. Our family foundation will be fully equipped to administer the endowment and will also have the flexibility to increase, decrease or eliminate funding if the trustees determine that the program no longer fits our mission parameters.

4. Community Foundation – A number of communities have foundations that will take gifts during your lifetime or after and deploy the funds as you direct. Perhaps you have a passion for your local zoo, your local symphony and your local art museum. You can create endowments for each of these causes to be administered through the community foundation. As with most third party situations (a university foundation, community foundation, etc.) there will be some administrative costs.

Learn to Receive

At the beginning of this chapter you were asked if you get more pleasure giving than receiving. I enjoy giving much more than getting. But I've also come to realize that receiving is an important part of the overall giving cycle. I used to get an almost euphoric sensation when I was the giver and an embarrassed feeling when I was the receiver. My minister helped me to understand that giving and receiving is a cycle and without allowing both to happen the process cannot be complete. Why does it really matter though if the cycle is complete? One reason is that we deny others the joy they feel when they give to us. Don't be confused that this cycle is specifically circular. Derive your pleasure from giving and be open and receptive when yet another person wants to give to you.

The Law of Attraction is another and even more powerful reason to learn to receive. All the positive energy you're generating; all the marvelous relationships you're building, and all of your generosity merges in an irresistible force. The Law of Attraction is inextricably linked to each of your thoughts and actions, and embodies the way you live your life. Thus, good things must and will come your way. Be ready to receive them with gratitude and a warm heart. To block the flow of good that is yours to receive upsets the balance that is inherent with the Law of Attraction.

Invariably as you "give it away," others may want to recognize you for your gifts. You must decide what level of recognition you're comfortable with. With most of our gifts we ask that there be no recognition or acknowledgement. That's our personal preference. There is nothing wrong with accepting recognition if your giving motives are pure.

For years I told the Dean of the College of Education that we didn't want recognition for our contributions to the teacher's scholarship program we had established. He respected our wishes for ten years. Then one day he invited my wife and me to honor his assistant on a Saturday morning. Little did we know he was planning to honor us. He assembled people we had worked with over the years at the university, the foundation and the College of Education and surprised us with a completely refurbished room bearing our name. For a fleeting moment, we were embarrassed because we felt we should focus on the wonderful students. Then I remembered the gift of receiving and was joyful and appreciative.

Make a Difference While You're Still Breathing

We've already discussed the giving of treasure while we're alive. Now let's talk about the gift of time and talent. You may be at a stage in your career that can't afford to give much more than your 10% tithe. But you can make a difference by giving of yourself in other ways. After all, the Law of Attraction isn't only treasure! How you offer your time and talent should be driven by your Vision and your giving strategy.

The time and talent I give is congruent with our Vision and is part of our strategy. For example, I have been heavily involved with my university foundation as a trustee, a member of the trustee's executive committee, chairman of the executive committee and chairman of the board of trustees.

I served on a search committee to identify a new president for our university and have chaired the College of Education Development Council since its inception.

With our teacher's scholarship program, we are active participants in selecting the recipients of the financial awards. For each incoming class of scholars, we host them individually with their parents in our suite for a football game. We print programs honoring each student; have a large sheet cake with their names on it. At half time, the dean drops by and we make a special gift presentation to the students. Hopefully, we make a life-long connection with those kids and their families.

My wife helps create, print and fold the weekly bulletin for our church. She retired after 29 years as a neo-natal intensive care nurse and enjoys giving of herself. The church staff loves to see her coming because she always brings homemade cookies and other treats. I serve on a prosperity committee at the church and also provide assistance to the facilities committee.

One of my most rewarding activities was that of mentoring other entrepreneurs. We are blessed to have a formal mentoring program in our community. Through this program, I've worked with individuals who are jazzed about building their businesses. I've worked with many entrepreneurs – either directly as mentees or assisting other mentors. For many years I have served on an advisory board for a woman whose company manufactures garments. And for nearly as long I've had weekly mentoring teleconferences with a very good friend who now lives in another city. My mentoring work isn't just about business. It's also about life, because for some reason we entrepreneurs tend to intertwine the two.

Mentoring has been very much an exercise in giving and receiving. I easily get as much out of the sessions as the mentees. These meetings stimulate new ideas that I can apply to my own businesses. The relationships that I have developed are rewarding beyond description. And I'm honored to watch people become believers in the Law of Attraction and to see their businesses grow.

There would be a huge hole in my life if I weren't able to give it away.

Action Summary

1.   Adopt tithing as one of your core principles. Give at least 10% of your income to the source that feeds your soul.

2.   Create a Vision for giving it away. Then develop a strategy to deliver your Vision.

3.   Don't get hung up on how much you have in the way of financial resources right now. Create your Vision and develop your strategy for the long haul.

4.   At some point, hire an attorney who specializes in estate planning.

5.   Learn to receive. It's part of the Law of Attraction. You are doing good things with your life and good things will come back to you. Let it happen!

6.   Let your Vision drive your giving of time and your talent.

7.   Know that you are creating a legacy of positive energy others will carry forward with the good work that you started.

I don't go looking for somewhere to spend my money. You can step on a tube of toothpaste for a week, if you have to. I spend what I need to and give it away.
~ T. Boone Pickens

CHAPTER 11

A Balancing Act

Balance your life – emotionally, intellectually, financially, physically, spiritually and with your family.

Have you ever been to a circus and watched the guy who sticks a pole on his forehead? On top of the pole are china plates, cups and other breakable items. This performer then rides a unicycle while juggling bowling pins, hatchets or even chainsaws. Get the picture? I have always marveled at what an amazing sense of balance these people possess. Without this balance . . . well it wouldn't be a pretty sight. Entrepreneurs are not always adept at life balance. We tend to throw ourselves into our work with gusto and to the exclusion of many others and other things. We excuse this by rationalizing that we're "sacrificing now for future rewards." (See Chapter One, *Be Alive*).

After a few years our lives have become patterned to be unbalanced. A life out-of-balance can manifest in many ways. We become one dimensional and may not be interesting to be around. Our health may suffer. We may experience extreme stress. We hit a slump. Our relationships may deteriorate. We may become less creative. We may miss irretrievable moments in our lives. Finally, we may miss an amazing opportunity because we weren't open and receptive to it (and totally unaware of it). Most of us probably would like to live a much more balanced life. But we don't know how.

An entrepreneur whose life is in balance has enhanced creativity and can find solutions to challenges more easily. A life in balance keeps stress at bay and helps to cultivate deeper and longer-lasting relationships. Positive energy flows continually. With balance, we avoid blockages in our heart and in our head.

Balance is a natural order. Maintain this natural order and everything is harmonious. Fail to do so and watch out! So, if balance is a natural order why do some of us fight it so hard? There are many explanations. See if the shoe fits with any of these:

> *"I have plenty of time to bring balance into my life."*

> *"I really truly love my work more than anything else."*

> *"I don't have the time to do anymore than I'm already doing."*

> *"I'm very happy with things just the way they are."*

What We Miss

Have you thought about all the things you might miss because your life is out of balance? Look at the following list and identify those activities or events that really don't mean that much to you.

1. Your child's first school play.

2. Spending time with your parents.

3. Watching the sun set over the ocean.

4. Your child's graduation from elementary school.

5. Your 20th high school class reunion.

6. A Christmas Eve candle lighting service.

7. Fishing with your son or daughter.

8. Taking a photo of a spectacular rainbow.

9. A special Valentine's dinner with your sweetie.

10. Lying in a hammock with a cool drink.

11. Reading a novel by your favorite author.

12. Enjoying a bottle of wine and your favorite music with friends.

13. Hiding Easter eggs for your grandchildren.

Form Life Partnerships

My partnerships force me to make a commitment to balance. You have to start from the premise that you really want your life to have an alignment of purpose. You have to believe that there's more reward to living a life of balance than there is risk. Once you accept this premise, you can move forward with creating your life partnerships.

The following diagram shows my committed partnerships.

Figure 1

Partnership Concept

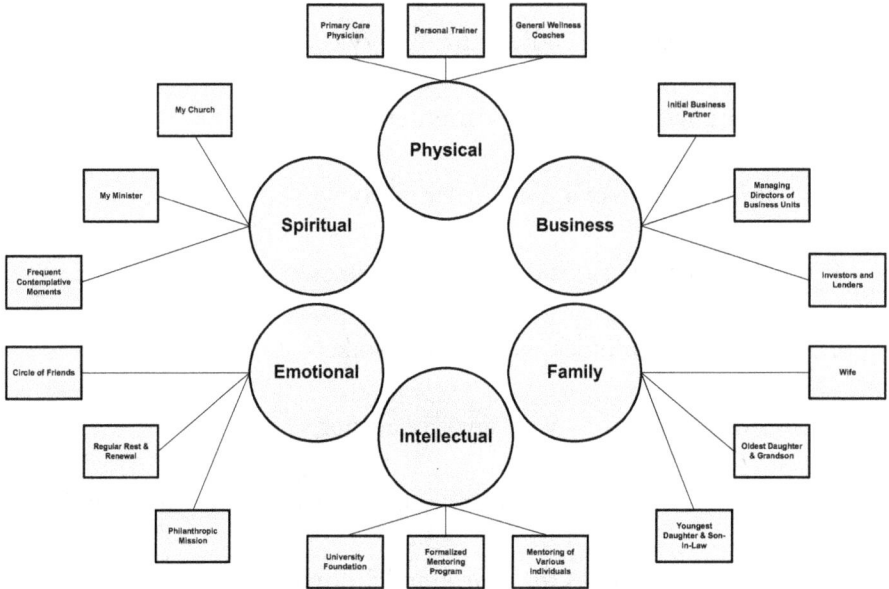

When you and another person or organization/institution enters into partnership, you are agreeing to establish and honor certain covenants. I recommend that you sit down with your partners and have an open discussion about what you want to achieve from this arrangement. Remember the WIIFM concept – what's in it for me. You need to benefit and so do your partners. Otherwise it's not a partnership. So, what you might consider a partnership really isn't one if all you do is take and give nothing to your purported partner.

I like to hold "partnership" meetings on a regular basis. For example, I meet quarterly with my minister to bring her up-to-date on what is going on in my business and personal life. I also ask her what I can do that helps her and my church community. I meet in similar fashion with my other partners. Where my family is concerned it is much less formal – but the commitment of time and energy is not diminished.

Your life partnerships provide ongoing and continuous support for you. I'm about the most Type "A" person you'll ever meet. But when I'm with my partners I let them support me. No longer do I have to slug it out completely on my own. We'll look at this in greater depth in the chapter entitled, *You're Not Doing This Alone.*

Vision and Priorities

In Chapter Two we discussed setting our Vision and Mission. A personal Vision will drive your priorities. And setting priorities helps balance your life. Take a look at your circles of influence – your physical health; your business and financial component; your family; your intellectual wellbeing; your emotional quotient and your spiritual influences. Establish priorities in each area. As entrepreneurs we know how to create strategic plans. Setting goals and objectives has become intuitive. Do the same for all elements of your life outside your business persona.

What might these priorities look like? Here are some ideas that may help you prime the pump.

1. **Physical**

    A. Develop an exercise routine that results in at least 210 minutes of cardiovascular support each week and at least another 90 minutes of weight training. *Potential Partner* – a personal trainer or an exercise buddy.

    B. Get an annual physical and do everything else that my doctor prescribes.

    C. Get seven hours of sleep each night. *Potential Partner* – you're on your own here.

D. Create and implement an overall wellness program. *Potential Partner* – chiropractor, massage therapist, acupuncturist and nutrition counselor.

2. **Business/Financial**

A. Develop a personal investment program to diversify your assets and generate the highest possible return with the lowest possible risk. *Potential Partner* – financial planner, investment manager.

B. Fund retirement accounts to the maximum allowable. *Potential Partner* – financial planner, investment manager.

C. Develop and maintain a comprehensive business strategy for your enterprise. *Potential Partner* – business partners and key employees.

D. Earn a specific dollar amount each year. *Potential Partner* – business partners and key employees.

3. **Family**

A. Keep work at work. *Potential Partner* – your spouse and children.

B. Have a "date night" each week with spouse. *Potential Partner* – spouse, of course.

C. Attend every school function for your kids. Potential Partner – your spouse and kids.

D. Take your family on at least two *non-working* vacations annually. *Potential Partner* – your spouse and children.

E. Have a "game night" with your family once a week. *Potential Partner* – your spouse and children.

F. Spend at least 30 minutes each evening reading to and playing with your kids if they are small. As they get older, spend this time helping them with their homework or talking with them about their lives. *Potential Partner* – your kids.

4. **Intellectual**

A. Read at least 50 books a year for pleasure. *Potential Partner* – join or start a reading circle.

B. Regularly read at least ten different newspapers and periodicals to broaden your view of the world. *Potential Partner* – you.

C. Attend one lecture, symposium or other event each month that is not related to your line of work. *Potential Partner* – a local college or university, civic organizations. You might want to find a friend who will do this with you.

D. Join one or two civic organizations that provide stimulation – political, economic development, service, etc. *Potential Partner* – civic organizations.

E. Learn a new language. *Potential Partner* – language coach or school.

5. **Emotional**

A. Volunteer for at least two hours each week. *Potential Partner* – local hospital.

B. Meet with friends at least once a week for dinner, a movie or some other form of fellowship. *Potential Partner* – circle of friends.

C. Pursue a hobby. *Potential Partner* – someone with a similar hobby interest.

6. **Spiritual**

A. Meditate at least 15 minutes daily. *Potential Partner* – you.

B. Tithe 10% of your income to the source that feeds your soul. *Potential Partner* – your church.

C. Attend a spiritual service every week. *Potential Partner* – your minister, your family.

D. Read at least one book each month that supports your spiritual quest. *Potential Partner* – your spiritual leader.

Become a Renaissance Man or Woman

Suppose you go to a cocktail party. Could you, over the course of the evening discuss:

1. What Vincent van Gogh was trying to express when he painted *The Potato Eaters* in 1885?

2. How many and who the current justices are on the U.S. Supreme Court?

3. The recent NBA game between the Lakers and the Celtics?

4. The Dow Jones Industrial Average?

5. The plot of the novel you are currently reading?

6. The plight of the Tibetan monks?

7. What causes an airplane wing to fly?

8. Doctrine of your church?

9. Your adventures from the vacation you took within the past 12 months?

If you lead a balanced life you will have a broad range of experience and knowledge. The word for the day is "curiosity." As a curious person you will constantly be seeking information about everything that is going on around you. If curiosity isn't your natural instinct, you can train yourself to become more interested in the world, by reading, Googling and talking to as many different people as you can about every subject you can think of.

The following thoughts were posted on the website www.artofmanliness.com in 2008 by Ross Crooks and Jason Lankow. It is one of the best compilations of ideas I've ever seen on the subject of becoming a Renaissance Man.

Every man should strive to reach his full potential. The competitive world in which we live stresses hyper-specialization as the way to get ahead. University graduate degrees narrow down a student's area of expertise to enable them fill a specific niche. Young boys are encouraged to choose a single sporting event in which they excel if they are to have any hope for a collegiate or professional career down the road. Sadly, this trend is slowly eliminating the once-popular aspiration of becoming a well-rounded man.

A gentleman should have a firm handle on not just one or two, but every aspect of his humanity, working to strengthen himself in every way possible. If he is blessed with the gift of intelligence, his academic pursuits should not be chased to the expense of his physical health. Similarly, a creative personality should not lead a man to isolate himself and ignore the social aspect of his being. Excellence in one of these areas does not take attention away from the pursuit of the others but rather serves only to increase competence in complimentary areas, giving man a greater understanding of himself and the world around him.

The ideal of the Renaissance Man originated in Italy, and is based on the belief that a man's capacity for personal development is without limits; competence in a broad range of abilities and areas of knowledge should be every man's goal and is within every man's grasp. What follows is a breakdown of the areas you need to master in order to become a true Renaissance Man.

Knowledge

The attainment of knowledge is central to one's development. A look at notable Renaissance Men throughout history makes it clear that this aspect is the most common and most extensive of all their aspirations. One must have a diverse knowledge of all academic fields in order to assure his competence. The traditional Renaissance Man was seen to possess not only a general understanding of many topics, but rather a display of expertise in at least two or more of these areas. Science, literature, mathematics, grammar, cultural history and politics are a good place to start.

Subscribe to periodicals that will stretch your scope of knowledge rather than limit it. Do not only peruse blogs that confirm what you already believe. If you must watch television, view programs that will sharpen your intelligence and wit while increasing your awareness of historical events and the current political landscape. Purchase a map of the world or globe and study it. Most people would be embarrassed by what they don't know when put to the test. Make a list of classic books, which you have not yet read, and schedule a time each day to start working your way down the list. Nothing exposes one's ignorance and lack of culture quicker than faulty geography or a lack of literary knowledge.

Subject yourself to material that is yet unknown to you, or opposes your current ideas. A lack of time is no excuse. Borrow from the library audiobooks on non-partisan politics, scientific developments, and religious practices of which you are somewhat or completely unaware and listen to them on your daily commute. Or tune into National Public Radio. This is essential to broadening your personal viewpoints, and will increase both your competence and confidence.

Physical Development

Not everyone possesses superb athleticism, but that is hardly an excuse to neglect the maintenance of one's physical self. Exercise of the body is every bit as important as that of the mind, and research shows that the two are actually quite complimentary. Leonardo da Vinci, whom many consider to be the ideal model of the Renaissance Man, was known to have been a brilliant scientist, inventor, painter, and musician. He was also said to have maintained an impeccable physique throughout his life.

Most people are not involved in physical activity as part of their livelihood, so it is an area that must be maintained by personal discipline. Develop a proper diet and moderate your intake of unhealthy food and drink. This is an essential part of everyone's health. You must set aside time every week for an exercise routine, be it running, cycling, or lifting weights. Find activities that you enjoy and that will not seem like drudgery.

Establish personal goals for distance or duration of your workout, and increase these goals as they are met. Work with others who have similar objectives and abilities to hold each other accountable for the routine. If you are not self-motivated at first, participate in community races or marathons in order to keep yourself responsible. The physical changes you will witness and the discipline you establish will surely have positive manifestations in all other areas of your life.

Social Accomplishments

A well-adjusted social life is perhaps the most important factor for one to maintain personal sanity and mental health. Not to mention the fact that strong interpersonal skills make a person an appealing candidate for both friendship and relationship. It is also a person's responsibility as a citizen to make a significant contribution to his or her community throughout the course of life, whether it be through time or money or both.

A person's social life begins with his or her own personality, an area that demands a great deal of attention and introspection. You must recognize what you have to offer to others and constantly work to increase your contribution. Hone your listening skills, for everyone wants to be heard. Become a strong conversationalist. This is a combination of taking interest in the lives of others while bringing something of interest to the table yourself. The former consists only of the realization of the intrinsic value of others. The latter is dependent on your knowledge of social issues and influences, as well as your ability to convey them in an appropriate manner by reading others' reactions. You will find that this personal development of charismatic demeanor may benefit you more than any other pursuit in your life.

Contribution to your community is also a vital part of maintaining a healthy social life. Whether this is involvement in local government, enrollment in the military, or investment of time in social work, it is a responsibility that every man should take seriously. Make sure you are aware of the happenings in society, both locally and nationally. Assess your personal strengths and find a way to use them to benefit the greater good. Coach a Little League baseball team, become a Scoutmaster, lend a hand at a homeless shelter, or organize a community event. This contribution and interaction as part of a group is a great way of developing yourself as a multi-faceted individual.

Arts

In our society, some view artistic pursuits as effeminate or limited to the elite class who possess the free time to engage in such frivolity (or alternatively, to those who have opted out of mainstream society and do not work). The Renaissance ideal is in sharp contrast to this mentality. Galileo painted and played the lute alongside his mastery of science and philosophy. Thomas Jefferson was an accomplished architect and designed innovative furniture and fixtures for his personal home throughout his illustrious political career.

A modern man or woman must recognize his or her creative self as an integral part of the whole. Knowledge of the Arts, as well as personal exercise of one's own form of expression prove important in personal development. Many people overlook their personal talents in this area because they are seen as less valuable or profitable than other strengths. Find an area of the arts that you enjoy and give it a go. Having trouble getting started? Many community colleges offer inexpensive art classes for beginners.

Many of history's greatest minds wrote poetry to express their visions that could not be conveyed in scientific findings or political theory. Pick up a pen and put it to paper, you may be surprised with the result. If you take particular interest in music or painting, use this as your means of expression. It will expand your mind and teach you more about yourself. The exercise of your creative side will likely prove an inspiration not only to yourself, but to others as well.

Jack of All Trades, Master of None OR True Renaissance Man?

As a result of the proliferation of knowledge and the creation of new fields and many subcategories within existing fields, it is impossible to have expert-level knowledge in all fields. And some may argue that those aspiring to extensive knowledge in a variety of fields do not ever master a field, and that only a few distinguished individuals can truly be polymathic Renaissance me and women. In truth, you may master that which you are passionate about, and yet aspire for competence in many areas. The true benefit comes in making the attempt, not in achieving perfection. By simply aspiring and seeking knowledge and wisdom in fields that impact all of our lives, you will become a better man, and certainly have a shot at being an indisputable Renaissance man or woman.

Uh Oh . . . Burnout

Burnout occurs when you feel overwhelmed and unable to meet constant demands. As the stress continues, you lose interest and motivation.

Stress vs. Burnout	
Stress	**Burnout**
Characterized by over-engagement	Characterized by disengagement
Emotions are over-reactive	Emotions are blunted
Produces urgency and hyperactivity	Produces helplessness and hopelessness
Loss of energy	Loss of motivation, ideals, and hope
Leads to anxiety disorders	Leads to detachment and depression
Primary damage is physical	Primary damage is emotional
May kill you prematurely	May make life seem not worth living

Source: *Stress and Burnout in Ministry*

Bringing balance into your life helps heal burn out. Creating your own "bucket list" of things you want to do helps you focus on partnerships and define your goals.

Action Summary

1. Form life partnerships in the areas of physical, business and financial, family, intellectual, emotional and spiritual.

2. Let your personal Vision and Mission drive your priorities in your life partnerships.

3. Become a Renaissance Person. Expand your horizons and broaden your knowledge in a wide range of areas and subjects.

4.   Create your own "bucket list" of things you absolutely do not want to miss during your lifetime.

Perpetual devotion to what a man calls his business,
is only to be sustained by perpetual neglect of many other things.
~ **Robert Louis Stevenson**

CHAPTER 12

PERSUADE AND COMMUNICATE

Help others buy your ideas.

Achieving your wildest dreams as an entrepreneur will most likely require interaction with other people. And when other people are added to the equation there will be a diversity of ideas and opinions. Your mission, should you choose to accept it, is to persuade others to see your point of view and move forward to deliver your vision. Some might call this salesmanship. I see it as more about helping someone make a buying decision. If you "sell" your ideas to someone you are the most active participant in the encounter. But if someone else "buys" your ideas, they become the most active participant and their purchase becomes much more "final." For others to buy your ideas you must be able to persuade and communicate – sometimes in very direct ways and at other times in more indirect manner.

We'll explore a few persuasion techniques. Let's create a hypothetical case study. As an entrepreneur, you need to raise $2 million in equity to launch a catfish farming operation. To succeed you'll have to make a compelling case for making such an investment.

Identify Your Audience

Who is your audience? Sometimes the shotgun approach does work. This is where you send information to a large number of prospective investors. I've found that mass marketing in fact is very effective in certain situations. And, I've learned that the rifle-shot method is equally effective – it just depends on the circumstances. The rifle-shot approach targets a small number of prospects based upon their likelihood to participate. In the case of raising capital for a catfish farm you need an investor who may have a unique investment philosophy. To find the person start networking in the following manner:

> ➢ Identify people who have invested in catfish farms.

> ➢ Talk with businesses that supply equipment and stock to catfish farms and see who they recommend.

> ➢ Talk to restaurant operators and seafood/fish wholesalers and get names from them.

> ➢ Speak with universities and agricultural extension services to see if they have any ideas.

Let's assume you identify three prospective investors. Now you need to learn everything you can about these prospective investors. Assume that two of them are repeat investors and one will be a first-time investor. Who are they? What other types of investments have they made? How many aquaculture operations have they funded? Naturally you will want to tailor and customize your presentation accordingly.

Build Relationships

Engaging in a "they buy" strategy means you'll first contact your targeted investors to begin building a relationship rather than plunging in with a sales pitch. Why? Because you have no idea what these investors need or want. You know little if anything about their investment or business philosophy. You don't know if you're compatible. After all, they will be your partners for a long time to come.

As a shrewd and enlightened entrepreneur you make contact with them. You tell them that you want to start a catfish farm and you are currently in the research phase. You understand that they have considerable experience (the two that are repeat investors) in catfish farming and you'd like to "pick their brains." It's flattering to be asked to share knowledge and it's a great way to start to build a relationship with your prospective investor. For the first-time investor, you tell him that you understand that he may be investing in a catfish farm and you wonder if he would share some of what he has learned about the business with you.

Meeting with the three prospective investors provides an opportunity for them to get to know more about you and for you to pick up some valuable tips about catfish farming. Your research is also a low-key way to gain a clear understanding of what makes these investors tick. You'll come away knowing what return on investment they desire; the length of their investment holding period; how they assess risk; how involved they want to be in managing their investment; what they are looking for in a partner, and a host of other factors. You gain a panoply of information and they become more comfortable with you.

Educate Your Audience

Now it's time to prepare your proposal.

> ➢ Provide a clear vision for your enterprise.

> ➢ Write a solid mission statement and articulate your core values.

> ➢ Prepare and include an Opportunities to Fail exercise and mitigate the risks (see chapter on *Risk*).

▷ Create a comprehensive business plan.

▷ Create a five-year financial forecast. For the first year, provide line item income and expense data. For the remaining years, show summary categories. Lay out your financial and operating assumptions so you anticipate their questions. You want your prospective investors to know that you have developed considerable knowledge about catfish farming, thus giving them comfort that their investment will be reasonably safe.

▷ Re-state their needs as you understand them and specifically make the link between your business and how it meets those needs.

Your proposal should educate the prospective investors about whom you are and why they should have confidence in you. It should educate them about the intricate details of your business idea. You want the educational process to do the selling for you.

Offer Choices

One of the best ways to encourage buyers to buy is to offer choices. Look for the alternatives within your business concept. Maybe there is more than one way to deliver your vision. Present those alternatives and let your prospective investor choose the most appealing option. This will make him an active participant in the buying process and he will feel as though he is more in control. For example, you could propose that the investor invest equity for a percentage interest in the company. Or the investor could buy preferred stock and receive a stipulated rate of return. The investor could have the right to convert his preferred stock into common equity. The ownership percentage would be different than if the investor bought a pure equity position at the outset. Allowing the prospective investor to choose between these two options may be instrumental in getting him to say, "Yes."

Appeal to Reason

Use factual evidence as proof for every premise you offer.

Your investors want numbers. They want to understand all of the risks and what you are doing to eliminate them. They want to know what sort of "skin" you have in the game. You'll win if you can show them that you have a solid plan that is based upon facts that you can prove. For example, if you project that your new company will increase its sales by 33% in the second year, show exactly how you intend to make this occur. Perhaps you can find data that shows that historically sales increase by 33% in the second year, of operation of a catfish farm. Or, maybe you have contacted a number of restaurant chains and have a commitment that they will increase their purchases (by 33%) in the second year of operation if you hold your price for 24 months. Presenting proof is one of the strongest methods of making a logical argument.

When making your presentation, litigation lawyer Paul M. Sandler, writing on legal ethos in the March 31, 2003, edition of the *Baltimore Business Journal*, recommends:

> ➤ Speak expressly in terms of the truth of what happened. By speaking of truth and fairness as shared values, you reinforce in your listener's mind your own adherence to these values.

> ➤ Be honest. For purposes of persuasion, perception of integrity matters.

> ➤ Admit unfavorable facts. When you are forthcoming about problems or weaknesses, you enhance credibility.

> ➤ Demonstrate your sense of fair play.

> ➤ Avoid taking extreme positions.

➤ Avoid asserting facts that your listener is unlikely to believe. If a listener thinks you are speaking falsely about any fact, your credibility will be undermined and your ability to persuade your listener about other facts or about the inferences to be drawn will be compromised. A statement is better omitted if your listener is not likely to believe it.

Features and Benefits

All too often entrepreneurs try to sell the sizzle without the steak . . . or in this case, the catfish. If you don't bring out a plate of succulent melt-in-your mouth catfish, you won't have any investors. Create a Feature/Benefit Worksheet for your idea. Suppose there are 20 features to your plan. You need to translate every single one of these features into how it benefits the investor. What are the benefits that are most important to them? How does your idea deliver those benefits?

Powerful Persuasion

Professor Robert Cialdini, Dr Noah J Goldstein and Steve J Martin wrote a book entitled, Yes, *50 Secrets from the Science of Persuasion*. In it they explain:

➤ When they think about persuasion, most people emphasize their own experiences rather than depending on data or techniques.

➤ Increase your persuasive power by understanding six core principles: "reciprocation", authority", "commitment/consistency", "scarcity", "liking" and "social proof".

➤ A small gift or favor will make you more persuasive. People will want to pay you back.

➤ The public believes in authority, so enlist higher-ups on your side.

➢ People want to be consistent and committed, so show how your proposal aligns with their values.

➢ The rarer something is the more people want it.

➢ Individuals want to be liked, so practice seeing the good in them.

➢ People tend to follow the majority. By establishing norms, you can get them to act as you wish.

➢ Fear paralyzes people, so use scare tactics only if you offer an antidote to fear.

➢ Admit your errors. Demonstrating honesty increases your influence.

Cialdini goes on to expand upon the following topics.

➢ **Reciprocation** – People tend to return a favor. Thus, the pervasiveness of free samples in marketing. In his conferences, he often uses the example of Ethiopia providing thousands of dollars in humanitarian aid to Mexico just after the 1985 earthquake, despite Ethiopia suffering from a crippling famine and civil war at the time. Ethiopia had been reciprocating for the diplomatic support Mexico provided when Italy invaded Ethiopia in 1937.

➢ **Commitment and Consistency** – Once people commit to what they think is right, they are more likely to honor that commitment, even if the original incentive or motivation is subsequently removed. For example, in car sales, suddenly raising the price at the last moment works because the buyer has already decided to buy.

➢ **Social Proof** – People will do things that other people are doing. For example, in one experiment, one person would look up into the sky; bystanders would then look up into the sky to see what they were seeing. At one point this experiment aborted, as so many people were looking up that they stopped traffic.

➢ **Authority** - People will tend to obey authority figures, even if they are asked to perform objectionable acts.

➢ **Liking** - People are easily persuaded by other people whom they like. Cialdini cites the marketing of Tupperware in what might now be called viral marketing. People were more likely to buy if they liked the person selling it to them.

➢ **Scarcity** – Perceived scarcity will generate demand. For example, saying offers are available for a "limited time only" encourages sales.

Effective Communications

Being an effective communicator is certainly a component of persuasion. A persuasive argument falls flat if the speaker is inarticulate or grammatically incorrect. Here are some tips to help you communicate (and thus persuade) effectively.

1. *Grammar, Syntax and Spelling* – If you aren't sure about a grammatical element of your communications, consult an online resource to help you determine if your usage is correct. Or find someone to edit and proofread what you have written or listen to a verbal presentation you plan to make. Most computer software for writing has a spell-check feature. While not right 100% of the time, it is still a valuable tool to help you improve the quality of what you write.

2. *Verbal Skills* – How often do you throw in the phrase, "you know" when you are speaking? How many "uhs" and "ums" are there? Have you mastered the art of intonation and voice inflection? Toastmaster organizations provide terrific support for someone wishing to speak more convincingly and persuasively. Visit the Toastmasters International website. If your speech pattern needs some help, consider

joining Toastmasters or hire a coach who can help you clean up your vernacular.

3. **Body Language** – Do you have nervous tics and gestures? Do you give away you innermost thoughts by the way you fold your arms or clench your jaw? Take a look at the following table for some ideas about positive body language.

NONVERBAL BEHAVIOR	INTERPRETATION
Brisk, erect walk	Confidence
Open palm	Sincerity, openness, innocence
Sitting, legs apart	Open, relaxed
Tilted head	Interest
Maintain eye contact	Attentiveness, interest
Hand to cheek	Evaluation, thinking
Smile	Friendliness
Maintain good posture	Confidence
Relax your shoulders	At ease
Nod when others speak	Interest

Action Summary:

1. You would rather have someone buy your idea or product, than for you to have to sell it to them. This will frame the process of persuasion in a totally different manner for you.

2. Determine which methods of persuasion work for you.

3. Identify and learn about your audience.

4. Build a relationship with your audience.

5. Educate your audience. Prepare a comprehensive and detailed proposal or presentation.

6. Offer choices designed to meet the potential investor's needs.

7. Use logic and factual information. Stay away from emotional arguments unless the situation calls for it specifically.

8. Present the features AND the benefits. Don't forget the WIIFM equation – What's In It For Me?

9. Be an effective communicator. Pay close attention to grammar, syntax, spelling, verbal skills and body language.

Persuasion is that all-important ability to get others to do what you want them to do because they want to do it. Maybe it takes reasoning, coaxing, explaining, or even a plate of brownies still warm from the oven. But whatever it takes, obviously persuasion is what's needed to make things happen, to take anything from Point A (your idea) to Point B (others helping to advance that idea).
~ Dr. Tony Alessandra

CHAPTER 13

YOU'RE NOT DOING THIS ALONE

You can't do this all by yourself. Develop a support network of colleagues, friends, family and a Higher Power.

There is an image from the Old West set against an orange sun on a hot, late-summer afternoon. And then you see him. The silhouette of a steely-eyed mustachioed gunfighter wearing a black hat, a long black coat and a six-shooter slung low on his hip. He moves slowly with spurs jangling but you know that he has catlike reflexes and could shoot the eye out of a buzzard at 200 yards. A chill runs up and down your spine as you realize that this guy doesn't need anyone else – he lives by his wits and his gun. This means he's not an entrepreneur.

There is simply no way that you can succeed as an entrepreneur without a support group. In an earlier chapter we discussed *Relationships*, primarily from a business perspective. In this chapter we'll explore how critical your personal support circle is to what you can accomplish. As much as you might fancy yourself as the lone wolf, the truth is that a number of the gunfighters were shot in the back. And that was the result of not having a support group to _watch_ their back for them.

Sometimes as entrepreneurs we feel that we have the weight of the world upon our shoulders. Periodically I feel a responsibility for my wife, my two grown daughters, my son-in-law, my grandson, my sister, my elderly mother, my elderly mother-in-law, my partners, my church, the employees of our various companies, my mentees and to some extent the rest of my family and friends. If I don't have my head screwed on straight I could go crazy worrying about all of these people.

Figure 1 below shows the support pyramid for each of us as entrepreneurs.

Figure 1
Support Pyramid

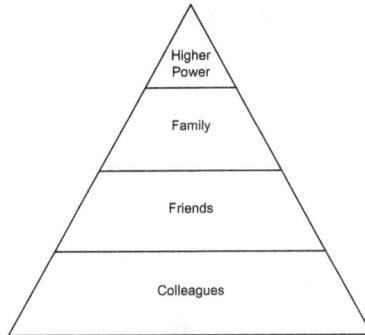

Colleagues

"Colleagues" refers to people we work with or are acquainted with through our business relationships. Often their support is purchased in the sense that they are compensated. This does not diminish the importance of their support, but it does create a different dynamic.

All too often entrepreneurs fail to acknowledge the support our colleagues provide. We are so intent upon reaching our objective that we completely miss the folks that are there, shoulder-to-shoulder with us making it happen. Common courtesies such as "please" and "thank you," drop by the wayside. Here's a little test.

1.   Has your assistant taken a vacation in the past year? If so, where did he or she go? What was the highlight of his or her trip?

2.   Has anyone with whom you work had a serious illness – either themselves or within their families? What was the illness? What was the treatment and what is the prognosis?

3.   Has anyone with whom you work recently experienced the death of a loved one? What did you do for this person?

4.   Pick three of your associates at random. Do you know what university they attended? In what field do they hold degrees?

5.   How many of your associates take work home with them? What sort of work? Why?

6.   Do any members of your team perform volunteer work within the community? Who are they and what do they do?

Now some entrepreneurs might say, "This is work and I pay those people to work. I'm not going to mix my business and social lives. But our attitudes toward our colleagues determine whether or not they see their work as a job or as a career. I prefer to work with people who want to be on my team for the long haul. I prefer to work with people who develop a passion similar to mine. I prefer to have people work "with" me and not "for" me.

The relationship we have with our colleagues should be one of caring, goodwill and appreciation. They may be paid to support our endeavors and adventures but they need more than money to really support our psyche and our soul.

Friends

How does a true friend provide support? The wife of a friend of ours was dying from brain cancer. A mutual friend (and one of my former partners) put his business on hold and flew to where she was lying in a hospice bed. He was there in an unconditional way to provide whatever assistance and support was needed during a very traumatic time. I have always admired him for this selfless act of true friendship. In another instance, a neighbor had recently adopted a baby boy. The new mother was overwhelmed and called my wife one evening in a moment of desperation. My wife walked across the street and helped our neighbor understand that sleep deprivation was the cause for her anxiety. This act of friendship provided the moment of clarity needed for our neighbor to get a grip on the situation and begin thinking clearly again. Friendships exist if we invest in them. We will only get out of them what we put into them.

The English novelist George Elliot (Mary Anne Evans) once said, "Friendship is the inexpressible comfort of feeling safe with a person, having neither to weigh thoughts nor measure words." And the Roman philosopher, Cicero, said, "Friendship makes prosperity brighter, while it lightens adversity by sharing its grief and anxieties." We entrepreneurs need to be a special kind of friend. Our lives tend to be a whirlwind of ideas and activities. Some of my happiest times are found in the midst of what must appear to be utter chaos to other people. Normal people (our friends) may feel uncomfortable with our pace and our multi-tasking. When I'm with my friends I slow my pace and stop my multi-tasking. I refrain from making or taking calls on my cell phone. I look them in the eye when I'm talking and fully acknowledge their presence. If I can't make this simple adjustment to my crazy lifestyle, how can I expect my friends to feel comfortable when around me?

Family

How should we use our family for support? First we must start with an understanding of what our families expect from us. They want our love and affection. They want our undivided attention. They want our words of encouragement, praise and strength. They want our integrity and our trust. They want our patience and our wisdom. They want our counsel and devotion. They want us to laugh with them and cry with them.

So we give them our support in all of these ways and as we give of ourselves we receive the same in return. We need to know our families love us. A deep and lasting relationship with your family is how this unconditional love develops.

Unlike other relationships, the family may be the most forgiving of our shortcomings as entrepreneurs. When the chips are down we need the support of our families more than from anyone else. A strong marriage or relationship with a significant other is crucial. Yet neglecting our spouse is a common malady suffered by entrepreneurs. We tend to take them for granted and then are arrogant enough to expect them to be standing by our side when we need them. Folks, it doesn't work this way.

So here's my advice. Make your family one of the most important focuses of your life. Do for them what you would like for them to do for you.

A Higher Power

Many people don't want to get into discussions about a Higher Power because they don't want to discuss religion. Perhaps it makes them uncomfortable or maybe they don't really know what they believe. But spiritual self is real whether or not you want to acknowledge it. I feel your spiritual self is a vital component of a balanced entrepreneur.

You don't have to be religious to be a successful entrepreneur. What matters is what you believe. "Believe about what?" you ask. And I say, "Believe what you believe." Does this sound like I'm talking in riddles? Well let me explain.

I believe there's a Higher Power at work in the universe. I believe this Higher Power is a source for all of the good in my life. How do I know this? Because I believe what I believe. I choose not to pray to or worship my Higher Power in a literal sense as may be outlined in the Bible. Instead, I believe my Higher Power is a form of divine energy that I can to tap into whenever I want. The energy from my Higher Power enlightens me and provides wisdom. My mind becomes a receptive channel for new ideas. When I get myself out of the way and let the energy of my Higher Power course through my being, amazing things happen. But when I try to do it myself without the flow of divine energy, I stub my toe. Over and over and over again.

As a result of these beliefs, I no longer take on stress in my life. My prosperity consciousness is thriving. I am healthy, alive and living every day in the now. When the energy is flowing I feel an endorphin rush and I see pure white light. I have clarity of purpose and my soul is fed.

What does this mean for you? Deon Du Plessis, author of *The Self Improvement Gym* writes, *"The greatest challenge is that many people define spirituality by religious connotations and religion is almost exclusively based on outward experience and conforming to someone else's rules."* He goes on to say, *"One of the most powerful and useful ways to define spirituality for yourself is to recognize and nurture that divine spark deep within you. As you grow in your understanding of this spiritual dimension you will be able to transcend the illusion of everyday awareness. Ultimately spirituality is about enriching your experience of life and to see a greater sense of meaning and purpose in life. Regardless of how you define spirituality, it is that still silent voice deep within. It is your spirit and it is your constant companion on life's journey. It is your own personal connection to the higher intelligence that's present in all of life."*

For the past 40 years I've been practicing the positive and practical way of life. I've learned how to become still and meditate. I've learned how to visualize the good things that happen in my life. I've learned to be more resilient, more patient, more loving, more generous and more forgiving. My Higher Power is my safe haven. Becoming spiritually aligned has made me a better husband, a better father, a better grandfather, a better friend, a better entrepreneur and a better person.

I hope that you will find your Higher Power. Your Higher Power doesn't have to be like my Higher Power or anyone else's. Somewhere along the line you have to realize that you're not doing this alone. Besides colleagues, friends and family, you also have the total and unconditional support of a

Higher Power – whatever it is. Ultimately you need to believe what you believe. But you **do** need to believe.

Action Summary

1. There is simply no way that you can succeed as an entrepreneur without a support group.

2. Develop a relationship of support with your business colleagues through caring for and acknowledging them.

3. Friendship requires an emotional investment. You need friendships as your next level of support. Set aside your daily activities when interacting with your friends and be there for them. When you need them they will be there in the moment for you.

4. The powerful support of family requires the greatest investment of all. It requires unconditional love. No matter what a member of your family might do, your love must remain constant.

5. The final element of support in your life is whatever Higher Power you believe exists. That's the key . . . believe. You believe what you believe, but you gotta believe.

> *I cannot imagine how the clockwork of the*
> *universe can exist without the clockmaker.*
> ~ **Voltaire**

Acknowledgements

I am indebted to many people who made this book a collaborative effort. I wish to express my appreciation to Barnett Helzberg who was kind enough to spend his time reviewing my manuscript and offering his wisdom as one of America's most successful entrepreneurs. Thanks also to my editor, Deborah Shouse from whom I learned much about my writing style (that hopefully improved in the process). My gratitude also extends to my wonderful friend Jenné Fromm who encouraged me to share my ideas and perspective.

Since 1975, my partner, Bob Esrey, has supported me in every way imaginable and enabled me to hone my entrepreneurial skills within our organization. Bob – thank you from the bottom of my heart. And since 1996, my partner, Jeanette Jayne, has helped me implement both the hair-brained schemes and a few rather good ideas. Thanks for your tireless efforts and your loyalty.

Finally, I owe the deepest of all my gratitude and appreciation to the love of my life since 1971. Barb Harris believed in me from Day One. She dreamt with me; rode the roller coaster with me; was the calm during all my storms, and walked beside me every step of the way. I love you Babe.

About the Author

R. Lee Harris grew up in Manhattan, Kansas and has lived in the Kansas City area since 1977. A 1975 graduate of Kansas State University, Harris began his career with Cohen-Esrey Real Estate Services, LLC, as an apartment manager two weeks after he graduated. Now president and CEO, he is involved in apartment management, development and investment; construction and tax credit syndication on a nationwide scale. Over the course of his career Harris has overseen the management of more than 27 million square feet of office building, shopping center and industrial space and nearly 60,000 multi-family units.

In 1991, Harris wrote a book entitled, *The Customer Is King!* published by Quality Press of Milwaukee. He has mentored a number of business people over the years and has been a long-time participant in the Helzberg Entrepreneurial Mentoring Program. He and his wife Barb have two grown daughters and one grandson. They are active in their church, community and university.